# The Battle of the River Plate

Campaign Chronicles

# The Battle of the River Plate

A Grand Delusion

## Richard Woodman

Campaign Chronicles
*Series Editor*

Christopher Summerville

Pen & Sword
**MILITARY**

The publisher and author would like to express sincerest thanks to John Morris for providing the line drawings used throughout this book; and to Geoff Green, who has made pictures from his Naval archive available for use in this book.

ISBN 978 184415 689 4

The right of Richard Woodman to be identified as Author of this Work has been asserted by him in accordance with the Copyright, Designs and Patents Act 1988.

A CIP catalogue record for this book is available from the British Library.

Typeset in Sabon by
Pen & Sword Books Limited

Printed and bound in England by
Biddles Ltd

Pen & Sword Books Ltd incorporates the imprints of Pen & Sword Aviation, Pen & Sword Maritime, Pen & Sword Military, Wharncliffe Local History, Pen & Sword Select, Pen & Sword Military Classics and Leo Cooper.

For a complete list of Pen & Sword titles please contact
PEN & SWORD BOOKS LIMITED
47 Church Street, Barnsley, South Yorkshire, S70 2AS, England
E-mail: enquiries@pen-and-sword.co.uk
Website: www.pen-and-sword.co.uk

# Contents

# List of Maps
# and Illustrations

MAPS

ILLUSTRATIONS

# Maps

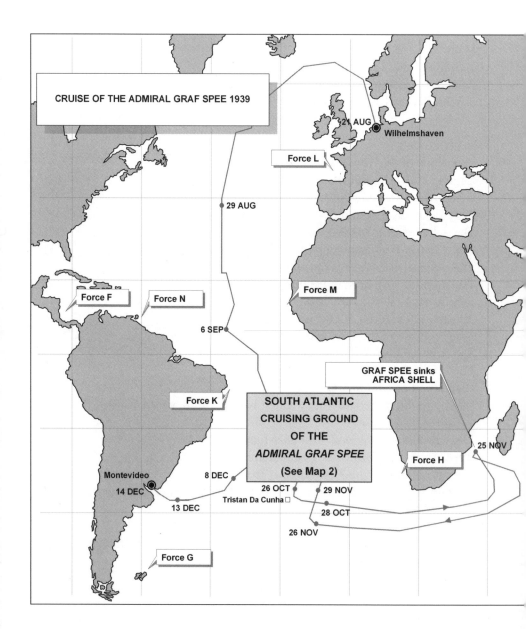

CRUISE OF THE ADMIRAL GRAF SPEE 1939

21 AUG
Wilhelmshaven

Force L

29 AUG

Force F

Force N

Force M

6 SEP

GRAF SPEE sinks
AFRICA SHELL

Force K

SOUTH ATLANTIC
CRUISING GROUND
OF THE
*ADMIRAL GRAF SPEE*
(See Map 2)

25 NOV

Force H

Montevideo

8 DEC

14 DEC

26 OCT

29 NOV

13 DEC

Tristan Da Cunha

28 OCT

26 NOV

Force G

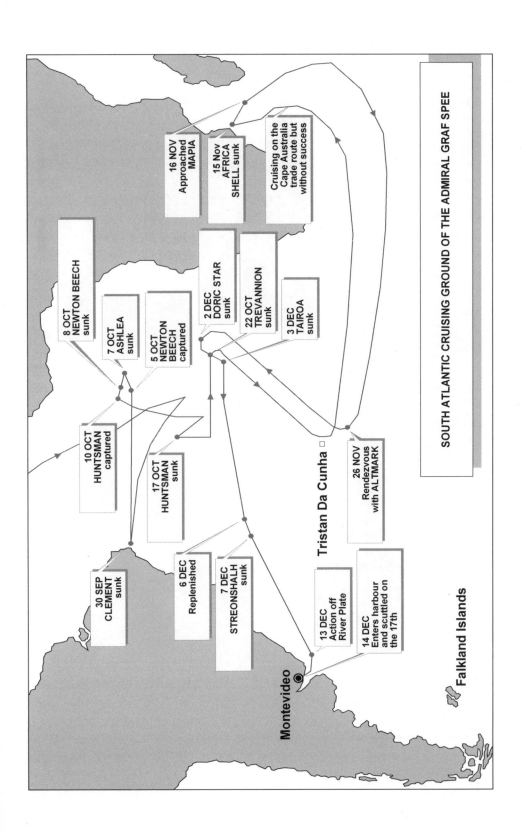

SOUTH ATLANTIC CRUISING GROUND OF THE ADMIRAL GRAF SPEE

30 SEP
CLEMENT
sunk

6 DEC
Replenished

7 DEC
STREONSHALH
sunk

10 OCT
HUNTSMAN
captured

17 OCT
HUNTSMAN
sunk

8 OCT
NEWTON BEECH
sunk

7 OCT
ASHLEA
sunk

5 OCT
NEWTON BEECH
captured

16 NOV
Approached
MAPIA

15 Nov
AFRICA
SHELL sunk

Cruising on the
Cape Australia
trade route but
without success

2 DEC
DORIC STAR
sunk

22 OCT
TREVANNION
sunk

3 DEC
TAIROA
sunk

26 NOV
Rendezvous
with ALTMARK

Tristan Da Cunha □

13 DEC
Action off
River Plate

14 DEC
Enters harbour
and scuttled on
the 17th

Montevideo

Falkland Islands

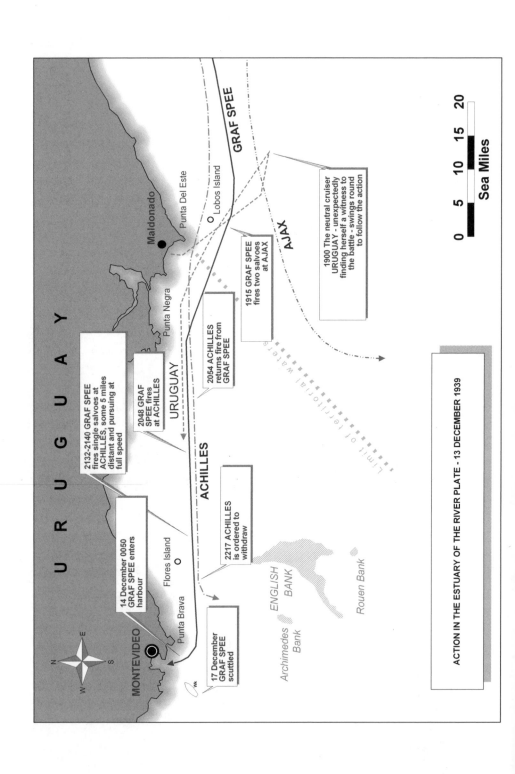

ACTION IN THE ESTUARY OF THE RIVER PLATE - 13 DECEMBER 1939

# Background

Sly Advance: The Cruise of the *Admiral Graf Spee*,
April 1928–August 1939

In order to fulfil its military definition a campaign has to secure its objective; like a good story, it has a beginning, a middle and an end, but unlike fiction, its aftermath is often long, sometimes profound and occasionally indistinct in effect. Moreover, since such events rely entirely upon the actions – both intellectual and physical – of human beings, they are inevitably composed of triumphs and tragedies. In so many cases, since war is composed of it, it is the tragedy that proves enduring. All these elements are present in the campaign under consideration: the cruise of the German commerce raider *Admiral Graf Spee*.

On the one hand the *Panzerschiff* was sent to sea with the blessing of the German High Command, whose directions to the *Oberkommando der Kriegsmarine* – the OKM or German Naval High Command – were quite specific: the wholesale destruction of enemy merchant shipping. On the other, the reaction to the raider's depredations was swift and overwhelming: a puissant mass of Allied naval power was mustered and dispatched in hot pursuit.

Early and confusing news of the *Admiral Graf Spee*'s interdiction of British merchantmen in those first weeks of war suggested that the British Admiralty's worst fears were realized. Despite the torpedoing of the British liner *Athenia* by a U-boat within hours of the British declaration of war on Germany, it was the heavy calibre guns of commerce raiders, able to operate at will far from the bases of the overstretched resources of the British and French navies that most concerned the staff officers in Whitehall. The deceptions adopted by

1

# The Battle of the River Plate

*Kapitän zur See* Hans Langsdorff – the disguises under which his ship made her attacks and the widespread locations of his strikes – unhappily coupled with the inability of Allied forces to pin down his whereabouts: circumstances that initially convinced London there were at least two of what the British called 'pocket battleships' at large in the Atlantic.

However, time was not on the German side. No German raider could operate undetected indefinitely. As Langsdorff pursued his objective to destroy enemy shipping, the countervailing campaign to annihilate him became, in time, a classic of cruiser warfare, redolent of all the old dash and élan of the Age of Nelson. Just as the Admiralty's worst (but traditionally rooted) fears seemed to come to pass, it knew exactly what to do. Thus had the eponymous German *Vizeadmiral*, Graf von Spee himself, having defeated the squadron of British cruisers under Admiral Christopher Craddock off the Chilean coast at Coronel in 1914, been hunted to destruction a few months later off the Falklands by a vengeful Sturdee. So too would Langsdorff be nailed.

Langsdorff, of course, famously never sank a British warship, nor did he kill a single British merchant seaman, but his *Panzerschiff*, with her solitary battle honour 'Coronel' upon her steel forebridge, sank 50,089 gross registered tons of British merchant shipping. In its own way, this was as great a stain upon the Royal Navy's reputation as any defeat in a fair fight between men-of-war, for it was the Royal Navy's primary – if unpopular – duty to protect the nation's trade, and thus sustain Britain's accelerated economy without which she had no means of waging war. This was a permanent axiom of naval faith, as Lord Nelson had known when writing to Captain Henry Blackwood in March 1804: 'the protection of our trade [is] the most essential service that can be performed'. In peacetime Great Britain relied upon the free passage of her merchant ships as the oxygen of her economic well-being; the more-so in war when, not only did she need to import additional commodities and war *matériel*, but she had to continue her trade in order to pay the additional costs of hostilities. This situation was exacerbated by the requisitioning of a number of merchant ships for state use: as military transports for troops and

2

# Background

military supplies, as hospital ships, as examination vessels to maintain a blockade of Germany and, perhaps most ironically, as Armed Merchant Cruisers, to sit amid a flock of merchantmen in convoy and defend her sisters against the anticipated attacks of German commerce raiders. In this they proved gallant but largely sacrificial, no match when they encountered the greater firepower and more accurately controlled gunnery of the *Admiral Graf Spee* and her two consorts, the *Admiral Scheer* and the *Deutschland*, let alone the fast battleships *Scharnhorst* and *Gneisenau*.

Despite the fact that, in addition to her First World War battle honour, the *Admiral Graf Spee* bore the Nazi *Swastika* and eagle upon her stern, neither the *Panzerschiff* nor her sisters had been built for the Nazi *Kriegsmarine*. They had, in fact, been constructed under the strictures and constraints of the Treaty of Versailles, allowing only a limited *Reichsmarine* to the Weimar Republic. The largest vessels allowed Germany were six 'armoured ships' for coastal defence, based on the Kaiser's pre-Dreadnought battleships. The calibre of their main-armament was decided, by subsequent negotiation between the Germans and the Conference of Allied Ambassadors set up to settle the detail of the Treaty, at 28cm (11 inches). A little more latitude was allowed under the Washington (Naval) Treaty of 1922 and the specification, not originally intended for commerce raiding on the high seas, but to defeat a French cruiser squadron in the Baltic.

Under the terms of a treaty between France and Poland, France was committed to sending such a force into the Baltic in support of her ally, whose territory obtruded into that of Prussia. German intelligence hinted that rather than a cruiser force, the French would augment their cruisers by the inclusion of the modernized *Voltaire*, whose main armament consisted of four 13-inch and twelve 9.4-inch guns, and various expedients were considered. None came to anything as Germany was overwhelmed by rampant inflation and civil discontent until in May 1925 Admiral Zenker, the new head of the *Marineleitung*, revived the project and more options were considered. However, any conclusion was hampered by French occupation of the steel-producing industrial area of the Ruhr until, in July 1926, the French withdrew, reinvigorating the matter.

# The Battle of the River Plate

By July 1927 prolonged consideration of several designs had reduced matters to four options of which Zenker selected a fast, small battlecruiser, protected by 100mm steel armour, mounting six 28cm (11-inch) guns and, at 27 knots, significantly faster than the heavier alternatives. The main calibre would not, it was rightly thought, cause great anxiety in the Allied admiralties, nor would the initial proposal for two such ships. To further head off Allied interest, Zenker insisted the proposed vessels be called *Panzerschiffs* – Armoured Ships – in conformity with the provisions of the Versailles Treaty. The Construction Office, under Dr Paul Presse, worked hard to draw up a thoroughly modern design, using where possible light metals and welding techniques to minimize weight and thus displacement tonnage which was restricted by the Washington Treaty. Also highly innovative were the eight, nine-cylinder, double-acting MAN diesel-engines, which occupied less room than steam plant. Moreover, although requiring a higher grade of oil than steam turbines, diesel-engines conferred great range on the new ships. Unfortunately, though compact, they saved little weight and compromise had to be sought in the armour, this being reduced from the planned 100mm, to variable 60–80mm plating. Despite their best endeavours, Presse and his team were unable to conform precisely to the 10,000-ton limitation, but the 1,700 overweight was not obvious; the projected design of April 1928 *looked* like a 10,000-ton ship and that was what mattered.

After a difficult passage through the *Reichstag* the first contract was agreed with the *Deutsche Werke* on 17 August 1928. All detailed drawings and specifications were completed before the end of the year, and the keel plates were laid on the slip at Kiel on 9 February 1929. By now, however, Zenker had become implicated in a scandal and had been succeeded by Erich Raeder.

Raeder was, from the beginning of his tenure of high command, opposed to war with Great Britain at sea: it could only result in humiliation for the German Navy. Besides, he saw the greater threat coming from France and he appears to have pinned his faith in the new *Panzerschiffs* operating not on the defensive in the Baltic, but on patrol in the North Sea, preventing any moves by the French to blockade the German coast.

# Background

A reprise on the Washington Treaty was held in London in 1930. The news of the new German ships stirred anxieties among the participants. Italy and France were agitated and sought to repudiate the Washington tonnage limitations. Mediating, Great Britain – which, alone of the powers had actually felt herself bound by the letter and not merely the spirit of the Treaty – sought to dissuade Berlin from a final decision to build until 1937. Germany sought a compromise, admitting her to the high table of naval negotiations, but this failed and the new-building went ahead. The vessel was launched on 19 May 1931, and named the *Deutschland*. Germany's ongoing economic difficulties delayed the laying down at the Marinewerft at Wilhelmshaven of the second *Panzerschiff* until 25 June.

Meanwhile, seeing the new German ships as a provocation, the French had taken the decision to build new ships and these were in turn considered to compromise the two *Panzerschiffs*. As the *Admiral Scheer* progressed, the matter of a third vessel occupied Raeder and his staff. With 3,000 skilled constructors jigged up for production and threatened with unemployment, another order had been placed with Wilhelmshaven on 23 August 1932. The keel plates of the third new man-of-war were laid on the slipway next to the second which, among other modifications, had increased beam and armour-plating.

On 1 April 1933 she was launched, named after Admiral Reinhard Scheer, hero of the Kaiser's High Seas Fleet. That same day the *Deutschland* was commissioned. A little earlier and prior to these naval celebrations the Nazi Party had come to power: upon her commissioning the *Deutschland* hoisted the *Swastika*.

The third *Panzerschiff* possessed several improvements over her predecessors. Her diesels were modified, smaller but heavier, her armour was thicker and incorporated 100mm transverse bulkhead at each end of the protected section. Her barbettes were heavily defended by plating up to 125mm thick, and her decking varied between 70 and 20mm depending upon location, with lower deck armour covering her magazines and with inclined anti-torpedo bulkheads fitted longitudinally. All this increased her light displacement to about 12,500 tons, considerably more when fully loaded with fuel, fresh water, stores and ammunition.

# The Battle of the River Plate

The splendid new ship was named after her father when launched by Huberta von Spee, rolling down the ways into the estuary of the Weser on 30 June 1934 to the cheering of a crowd of well-wishers. Towed to the fitting out berth, construction work went on. In November the *Admiral Scheer* was commissioned; the *Admiral Graf Spee* followed on 6 January 1936, when *Kapitän zur See* Konrad Patzig took command. She proved the fastest and most economical of the three sisters, making 28.5 knots on trials, driven by her twin screws.

Though not long, by the standards of the day, the 71-foot beam made the *Admiral Graf Spee* a stable gun platform, maximizing the potential of her newly designed twin triple-mounted turrets. At 40 degrees elevation, the 28cm weapons could throw a shell 36,475 metres, a little over 18 nautical miles, but they needed to drop back to 2 degrees of elevation for reloading, which would slow the rate of fire in an engagement. Secondary armament consisted of eight, singly mounted 15cm (5.9-inch) guns with an extreme range at 35 degrees elevation of 22,000 metres, about 11 miles. Anti-aircraft armament was provided by three twin 9cm (3.5-inch) guns, four twin 37mm calibre weapons, and eight 20mm guns. In addition to the guns, there were two quadruple torpedo tubes mounted on the quarterdeck and large searchlights were also fitted.

*Admiral Graf Spee*

# Background

Gun control was backed up from three positions and fitted with high-quality optical stereoscopic rangefinders, the primary one 10 metres in length. The acquired data was processed in the transmitting station below the forebridge, or conning tower, where it was mechanically converted and back-up facilities were provided.

As Dr Eric Grove points out 'Doctrine for the use of the armament was that both main armament turrets should engage a single target, firing single-turret three-gun salvos every ten or twelve seconds to obtain the range as quickly as possible. All German sources,' Grove assures us, 'insist on this point'. He adds that: 'While this was going on, the secondary armament could engage a different target if desired.'

Although a powerful ship – and she was to prove an efficient commerce raider – there remained flaws in her conception that made her less formidable than either the official designation of *Panzerschiff*, or the slightly mocking soubriquet of 'pocket battleship' might suggest. In fact only her barbettes and gun houses were fully armoured, while her hull-belting was more reminiscent of a cruiser's protection, so that she is best thought of as a very heavy cruiser and that, ultimately, was the role fate was to cast her in.

There were other flaws: her diesel engines – which, admittedly, gave her vast range – were to prove troublesome, creating vibration and occasional failure, while the heavily loaded hull possessed inadequate reserve buoyancy in having little sheer. In the event she proved wet in heavy weather, making her lower conning positions untenable in such conditions. Following tank-tests, modifications were planned but matters were gaining a momentum beyond the control of *Grossadmiral* Raeder and his staff. Although docked for a refit in 1938, alterations were superficial: an increase in AA calibre from 9 to 10.5cm (4.1-inch) weapons, removal of three of her searchlights and the fitting of *Seetakt*, an embryonic radar range-finding system, which remained inferior to the ship's superb optical equipment. More fundamental changes were never carried out, for the euphoric march of Hitler's Germany was under way.

Having joined the fleet on 9 May the *Admiral Graf Spee* anchored as flagship among the ships assembled for review in Kiel Bay at the

## HANS WILHELM LANGSDORFF
### 20 March 1894–19 December 1939

Born in the town of Bergen in the centre of the Baltic island of Rügen, Hans Langsdorff was the eldest son of Ludwig and Elizabeth Langsdorff. The family's males traditionally became pastors or lawyers, but a move to Düsseldorf, where his father was appointed judge, brought the young Hans into contact with Maximilian, *Reichsgraf von Spee*. The influence of the man who was to become a national figure during the First World War was profound, and Hans defied his parents to enter the Kiel Naval Academy in April 1912 as an officer-cadet. He passed out top of his entry and on joining the German Navy became a torpedo specialist, being appointed torpedo officer in the cruiser *Medusa*. By May 1916 Lieutenant Langsdorff was serving aboard the battleship *Grosser Kurfurst*, distinguishing himself at the Battle of Jutland and meriting the Iron Cross, 2nd Class.

end of the month. After this she headed out into the Atlantic, visiting the Canary Islands before entering the Mediterranean in pursuit of German foreign policy, protecting German interests and supporting Franco's fascist forces against the democratically elected Republican government in the Spanish Civil War. Unlike her sister-ships her five Spanish forays were relatively uneventful and between them, on 20 May 1937, she lay at anchor at Spithead, representing the resurgent Germany at the Coronation Review of King George VI.

Five months later Patzig handed over command to Walter Warzecha, who took her into Norwegian waters before completing the ship's service off Spain. Another training trip to Norway occupied the summer of 1938, which culminated in a further review at Kiel. Then, on 1 October, with the news of the Munich Agreement still fresh in everyone's mind, Warzecha was relieved by *Kapitän zur See* Hans Langsdorff.

Langsdorff took his ship into the Atlantic on a further training cruise, showing the flag at Vigo, Tangier, Bilbao and Lisbon. After an operation

# Background

Later that year Langsdorff was appointed to command a minesweeper and, a coming man, rose to command a flotilla. His reputation, popularity, skill and social graces ensured that, despite Germany's defeat and the consequent social upheaval which followed, Langsdorff survived the demise of the Imperial Navy to be promoted *Korvettenkapitän* in the new republican *Reichsmarine*. Now in his early thirties, Langsdorff enjoyed staff-appointments and throve under the new Nazi regime. Prior to his appointment to the *Admiral Graf Spee*, he had commanded a flotilla of large torpedo craft in Spanish waters. A contemporary colleague said of him that his intellect was 'far above the average', while 'his calm and well-balanced personality, together with his keen sense of humour and his tactical and strategic training' enabled him to 'master the hard task set him'.

in the Baltic in the following spring, when all three sister-ships threatened Memel, the *Admiral Graf Spee* was back in the Atlantic, flying the flag of Admiral Böhm and in company with three cruisers, seven destroyers, three U-boat flotillas and their tender; later they were joined by the *Deutschland*.

Finally, before returning to Germany at the end of May, Langsdorff's *Panzerschiff* escorted the Kondor Legion on its homeward passage after its notorious air-intervention in the Spanish Civil War. With Fascist leaders ensconced in Italy, Germany and the Iberian peninsula, and the British under Chamberlain content with their piece of paper, it was presumed that peace would prevail.

# Campaign Chronicle

While the Munich Crisis created an illusion of a peaceful future in Paris and London, German plans for expansion eastwards never wavered. As Hugh Trevor-Roper points out: 'Hitler was determined, one way or another, *so doer so* (in his own favourite phrase), first to break the Versailles Treaty which gave to the frontiers of Eastern Europe the guarantees of the Western Powers [. . .] and secondly, having thus secured his own rear, to hurl his armies [. . .] against Russia. He thus hoped to restore [. . .] at the very least, the frontiers of 1917, the frontiers achieved by the victorious armies of the Second Reich . . .'

This was the quest for living space – *Lebensraum* – for a revitalized and expanding Third Reich. Having smashed the Tsar's armies, there seemed no reason why German forces could not repeat the process and destroy the Red Army. Hitler's first objective was Germany's eastern neighbour, Poland, and, at least in the short term, he had secured a pact with Soviet Russia. After the German seizure of the greater part of Poland, the Russians would occupy the east of the country but, before this grand plan could be put into effect, Hitler must needs secure his rear. The Western Powers, France and Great Britain, had proved more or less supine over the reoccupation of the Rhineland, carried out after the French withdrawal in 1936. The annexation of Austria accomplished by the *Anschluss* of 1938 had raised little objection and the matter of the Sudetenland, a largely German populated province of Czechoslovakia had, Hitler thought in 1937, been 'written-off' by Britain and France. By a mixture of threat, diplomacy and deception Hitler intended to pursue his course – hitherto successfully having avoided outright war – manoeuvring Poland into a choice between siding with Germany or Russia, confident that the Soviet model would find little appeal among the Poles. While Poland might thus be subjugated an eventual war with Russia loomed as inevitable, 'A Cyclopean task' Hitler assessed, achievable only by 'the hardest man in centuries'.

To these ends the Nazi state had been harnessed from Hitler's assumption of the Reich Chancellery. That an undesirable war might have to be fought in the West had occurred to Hitler, though he thought and hoped it might be avoided, indeed he thought that British imperial interests would lead to a free hand being given to Germany, particularly if she took on the Red Menace of Communism posed by Stalin's Soviet Union. Moreover, he had told *Grossadmiral* Erich Raeder, then planning a new German Navy designed to wrest command of the seas from Britain, that a war with the British Empire, if it was to be embarked upon at all, would not be contemplated before 1944.

But in the summer of 1939 it became increasingly clear that although Hitler had diplomatically outflanked the Western Powers at Munich, a rumbling opposition to his threats and manoeuvres against Poland went on, compelling him to seek his pact with Moscow. This, his foreign minister von Ribbentrop triumphantly snatched from under the noses of Western diplomats trying to achieve the same objective. However, it was increasingly obvious that to avoid a showdown Hitler must seize Poland by a quick military campaign, compelling the Western Allies to accept what they would prove powerless to prevent. Experience suggested to Hitler that confronted with such a *fait accompli* neither Paris nor London had the will to go to war.

Thus, confident in continued military passivity from the West, and having stamped a new and personal command structure upon the German armed forces, Hitler began a war of nerves with Poland, which culminated in the creation of conditions on the frontier with Poland that made a German invasion appear as intervention in protection of German interests. With this *ruse de guerre* Adolf Hitler precipitated the second great tragedy of the twentieth century.

# The Battle of the River Plate

**5 August–29 September 1939: 'The Curtain Lifts'**
In his first War Directive, dated 31 August 1939, Hitler stressed the importance of leaving 'the responsibility for opening hostilities unmistakably to England and France', adding that should either country begin operations against Germany, German forces should simply hold the frontier and do nothing to compromise the defeat of Poland. Specifically, however, 'The Navy will operate against merchant shipping, with England as the focal point . . .' In fact contingent operations had already begun in late July, placing German naval forces in a position to respond to any hints that Britain might rally in support of Poland and to remove key units from the remote possibility of any enforced British blockade.

Secretly therefore, on 5 August, the German naval tanker *Altmark*, commanded by *Kapitän zur See* K.H. Dau and loaded with stores, food and ammunition, left Wilhelmshaven. The following day, in brilliant sunshine, she passed through the Strait of Dover, word of which was passed to the Admiralty, a first twitch of the curtain as it lifted upon the drama. The *Altmark*, a grey, black-funnelled tanker, was not a German-registered merchant ship, instead she flew the distinctive ensign of the Reich Service and was government owned. She doubled the South Foreland and Dungeness, then headed west, out of the Channel and across the North Atlantic, bound for Port Arthur on the Texan coast. Here she was to load 9,400 tons of diesel oil, ostensibly consigned to Rotterdam, but in truth to be held ready to operate in support of the *Admiral Graf Spee*.

*Altmark*

# 5 August–29 September: 'The Curtain Lifts'

The *Panzerschiff* herself was recalled from torpedo-firing exercises for a dry-docking on the 17th. While her bottom was cleaned and anti-fouled she was topped up with operational stores and a team of cypher decoding specialists from the *B-Dienst* service joined the ship, with some officers of the German naval reserve – men whose normal service in merchant ships had acquainted them with British trade routes, the nature of British-flagged shipping to be found on them and the familiarity to distinguish rapidly the identity, type and even the name of ships the *Admiral Graf Spee* would encounter.

Meanwhile, to augment this, on 19 August five U-boats sailed from Kiel, with a further nine leaving Wilhelmshaven; they had all been allocated 'waiting positions' in the North Atlantic.

Then, in the late afternoon of the 21st the *Admiral Graf Spee*, under the command of *Kapitän zur See* Hans Langsdorff, slipped seawards from Wilhelmshaven, heading north, to pass by way of the Iceland Faeroes Gap into the vast wastes of the Western Ocean. Two more U-boats, one of which was *U-30* commanded by *Kapitänleutnant zur See* Fritz-Julius Lemp, and a second fleet-tanker, the *Westerwald* under *Fregattenkapitän* Grau, followed. She was intended to operate in support of *Kapitän zur See* Wennecker's *Deutschland*, which left on 24 August and headed for a station off Cape Farewell, the southern tip of Greenland. Should any reaction emanate from London as events east of Germany unfolded, a show of muscle along Britain's vaunted sea frontier might achieve a similar climbdown as had the Führer's blandishments at Munich, but Hitler had taken no such precautions in the events leading to the Munich Crisis of 1938. In the operational orders issued to Langsdorff and Wennecker on 4 August it was clearly stated that: 'The political situation makes it appear possible that, in the event of a conflict with Poland, the Guarantor Powers (England and France) will intervene', and the *Luftwaffe* had been ordered to take advantage of any 'favourable opportunities to make an effective attack on massed English naval units, especially on battleships and aircraft carriers'.

By the 25th, as the hours were counted down to the invasion of Poland, Norddeich Radio had transmitted a warning to all German merchant ships, alerting them to the possibility of war. The danger of

British interception of German merchantmen on the high seas was critical. Two days later a second message followed, urging all merchant shipping to reach the Fatherland within four days, failing which they should head for a neutral or pro-German friendly port.

However, alarmed by intelligence, the British began seeking assurances that no military operations were in train. In Scapa Flow, the Royal Navy's anchorage in the Orkney Islands, the Home Fleet was ordered to raise steam. Under Admiral of the Fleet Sir Charles Forbes the battle squadrons slipped their moorings and headed seaward in a show of strength and determination. Britain's traditional first weapon of defence was already mobilized. Hitler faltered as the possibility became a probability, postponing his invasion; but he was unable to stay his hand for long. German forces began their advance into Poland at dawn on the 1st September; that evening a first British ultimatum was delivered from London. During the 2nd, as the overwhelmed Polish forces fought valiantly, refusing to cave in, intense diplomatic activity sought to halt Hitler. Then, on the morning of the 3rd, Great Britain and France rallied to their Polish ally and declared war.

While Forbes was ordered to carry out a sweep in the Iceland/Faeroe Gap in search of German merchant ships, particularly the liner *Bremen*, and HMS *Somali*, Captain Nicholson, of the 6th Destroyer Flotilla captured the *Hannah Boge* 350 miles south of Iceland, the waiting *Panzerschiffs* and U-boats, by a conspicuous and swift interdiction of British merchant shipping, might still prevent a declaration of war in support of a dying ally amount to full-blown hostilities. But then, on the very evening of the day on which a betrayed Neville Chamberlain had declared Britain and her empire at war with Germany, Lemp sank the British passenger liner *Athenia* off Malin Head.

Hitler had expressly forbidden the sinking of passenger liners and although Lemp was afterwards exonerated from charges of disobedience on the grounds that he believed the *Athenia* to have been an Armed Merchant Cruiser, the attack convinced the Admiralty that the Germans had embarked on unrestricted submarine warfare. Although initially far from perfect, merchant shipping was immediately organized in convoy, as much against the firepower of surface raiders, *Hilfskruizers* (fast cargo liners heavily armed as commerce raiders) and *Panzerschiffs*, as against the torpedo of the U-boat. But convoy could only be extended across the North Atlantic and south to Gibraltar and Sierra Leone. British merchantmen, owned by hundreds of private shipping companies, traded worldwide. For a sea officer of the Third Reich determined to interdict the enemy's supply routes, there were opportunities galore not in the North, but in the South Atlantic.

In contact – but not in company – with Dau, Langsdorff headed south for his 'waiting station' off Pernambuco (modern Recife) on the shoulder of Brazil but adjacent to the so-called Atlantic Narrows.

*Grossadmiral* Raeder had prepared his small but modern navy for a war on trade to the best of his ability and in spite of the shortfall in time the Führer had assured him he would have. He knew, as Stephen Roskill pointed out after the war, that: 'The effectiveness of surface raiders depends not only on the actual sinkings and captures which they accomplish but on the disorganization to the flow of shipping which their presence, or even the suspicion of their presence, generates'. Raeder's first principle was, therefore, concealment; his second deception. Langsdorff and Wennecker were expected to take advantage of the vast areas of open ocean uncrossed by the traditional trade routes and far beyond the reach of air reconnaissance. It would be in such wild spots that the *Panzerschiffs* would rendezvous with their supply tankers. For the *Admiral Graf Spee*, a cruising ground in the South Atlantic had been chosen. Here two major British supply routes offered alternative targets. The route from the Rio de la Plata, much favoured by fast, frozen meat-carrying ships, would prove one area rich in pickings. The other, to and from the Cape of Good Hope, not only exposed the traffic to Cape Town, but also some services from Australia and India which, by taking in East African ports, favoured the Cape route rather than the transit of the Suez Canal. Not only did these twin major arteries of British imperial trade allow Langsdorff a choice of targets, but they could be struck anywhere along their attenuated lengths. He was to avoid their concentrated choke-points, for at such foci strongest naval protection would most likely be found. But both routes bore a mass of shipping, from the fast reefers, mentioned earlier, to the equally fast passenger and mail liners, cargo liners with valuable ladings of outward general cargo and homeward loads of produce from all over the world including tanks of Tung and palm oils, latex and tallow. There were also the heavily burdened tramp ships with their homogenous bulk cargoes of coal, steel, sugar, wheat, iron and manganese ore, loads of flax and rubber, their deck-cargoes of flammable esparto grass and timber. Nor did these ships trade directly between Great Britain and her partners, but provided shipping services to other nations. Disruption of these would have wider political implications detrimental to invisible earnings for the British economy. Moreover, to throw any pursuit off his trail, Langsdorff could disappear into the Southern Ocean and double either of the great capes, to reappear in the Pacific or the Indian Oceans, or to descend on the British and South African whaling fleet in the waters south of the Falklands. As his operational orders summed up: 'The enemy is not in a position to carry his complete import requirements in escorted convoys. Independent ships can therefore be expected.'

Although specifically ordered to obey the Hague Convention and respect the Prize Regulations applied to cruiser warfare against unarmed civilian merchantmen, Langsdorff was to strike and withdraw, to keep the enemy guessing, to disguise his ship by means of wood, canvas and paint. The hoisting of neutral naval ensigns as they approached a victim was approved under international law, provided the belligerent ensign was run up prior to fire being opened. Above all, Langsdorff was to avoid any contact with British naval forces. If these should be encountered by accident and 'even if inferior, [they] are only to be engaged if it should further the principal task (i.e. war on merchant shipping)'. This, Langsdorff was to discover, was not merely more difficult than the staff officers in the *Seekriegsleitung* supposed when drafting his instructions, but would prove the very crux of the matter and the cause of his undoing.

His master, Erich Raeder, sensed this, and presciently wrote a reflection on the situation on 3 September, the very day that war broke out. Of his surface forces, the *Grossadmiral* said that they could 'do no more than show that they know how to die gallantly . . .' Specifically the achievements of the *Deutschland* and the *Admiral Graf Spee*, 'if skilfully used, should be able to carry out cruiser warfare on the high seas for some time'. He added, just before he asked *Korvettenkapitän* Heinz Assman to countersign the document: 'The *Panzerschiffs*, however, cannot be decisive in the war . . .'

Despite – or perhaps because of – these misgivings, Raeder had given his commanders the greatest possible latitude, allowing them the untrammelled judgement of the man-on-the-spot. Moreover, by way of encouragement, provided 'operational possibilities were exhausted' they might, in extremis, run into a neutral port where, however, they must 'without fail [. . .] ensure that on no account the ship falls into enemy hands'. Having held out the carrot, Raeder could not conceal the stick: 'I shall act without mercy against any commander who compromises the honour of the Flag and is found lacking in that energy which alone can bring success and achieve a position of respect for the *Kriegsmarine*. Rather death with honour than strike the Flag!'

*

Langsdorff's escape undetected into the Atlantic was a model of careful navigational passage-planning, hugging the Norwegian coast as though on an exercise, taking a wide sweep north of Fair Isle and the Shetlands and passing through areas where shipping might be encountered during the hours of darkness. In this he was fortuitously assisted by a suspension on the 21st of the North Sea air patrols which had been a feature of British naval exercises during August. On the 23rd the *Admiral Graf Spee* was north-west of Bergen, she then slowed down until, on the 24th off Stokksnes, Iceland, she increased speed and swung south and west. Four days later, east of Cape Race, Newfoundland, she was heading due south, to meet the *Altmark*. Securing to a line trailed astern of the tanker, they passed a hose and topped up with fuel. Some unwanted material was disposed of and two 20mm guns were transferred to the tanker for her own defence. The two ships then proceeded south in company, sing-songs being organized to raise morale so that, by Sunday, 3 September, the *Admiral Graf Spee* was north-west of the Cape Verde Islands, adjusting her speed and making small and local alterations of course to avoid being seen by any merchantmen.

The first positive news of war came from a *B-Dienst* intercept of the BBC's broadcast from Rugby. Langsdorff had forbidden his officers to listen to the BBC but the German signal notifying them of war arrived within the hour. Soon afterwards came an instruction not to attack French shipping – by which his ship would assuredly be reported – in an attempt by Hitler to divide the Western Allies. *B-Dienst* intercepts also informed him that British naval precautions were in hand, convoy arrangements were already made and naval forces were being built up at Freetown, Sierra Leone, the southern rendezvous point for North Atlantic convoys. Finally, further disheartening news came in the wake of Lemp's precipitate action in sinking the *Athenia*: the immediate organization of convoy, but the otherwise quiescent attitude of the British and French persuaded Berlin – still trying to avoid a hot war with Britain – that commerce raiding was 'inadvisable at present'. Maintaining radio silence the *Admiral Graf Spee* was to move father south, to 'hold back and withdraw . . .'

Three days later, midway between Freetown and Trinidad, she altered course south-eastwards to her new 'waiting position', a vast scalene triangle with its dart-like and shallowest angle pointing at the Cape of Good Hope many miles away, but lying between the two major trade routes in the South Atlantic and where she and the *Altmark* arrived on 10 September. The two ships ran under reduced engine revolutions, biding the outcome of events upon the plains of Northern Europe. On 11 September Langsdorff secured his isolation by flying-off his Arado 196 floatplane to provide notice of any shipping and, with boats ferrying stores between the two ships, began a replenishment from the *Altmark*. While this was in hand the Arado sighted two vessels one of which they thought to be a British cruiser. To their horror it appeared to alter course and to head for the position of the *Admiral Graf Spee* and her consort. Hoping his aeroplane had gone unobserved but maintaining radio silence, the

Arado pilot banked steeply and headed for home.

Immediately on receipt of this intelligence, Langsdorff aborted the replenishment and, recovering his boats and the Arado, sped away; Dau took *Altmark* on a diverging course. The alarm had been caused by HMS *Cumberland*, on her way from Plymouth to reinforce Commodore Henry Harwood's cruiser squadron then off Rio de Janeiro. The abrupt and purposeful alteration of course had been merely a routine change from zig to zag as the *Cumberland* carried out standard anti-submarine procedure along a median rhumb-line. Langsdorff had no such comforting assurance, however, and his *B-Dienst* people were put to the task of diligent interception of British naval signals to discover whether or not their presence was known to the enemy.

Meanwhile, far away Hitler and the *Oberkommando der Wehrmacht* vacillated over what to do next. On the 23rd the Führer, Keitel, Raeder and their respective staffs met at Zoppot to consider the situation vis-à-vis the Western Allies. Insofar as the *Deutschland* and the *Admiral Graf Spee* were concerned it was appreciated that, despite the support of the *Westerwald* and *Altmark*, their supplies were finite and they could not be asked to remain undetected indefinitely. There was also the awkward question of morale. Against this the second wave of U-boats would shortly be sent to sea and therefore an intensification of 'war against merchant shipping' should be initiated 'at the beginning of October'. To this the Führer agreed. Accordingly, on 26 September, the *Deutschland* and the *Admiral Graf Spee* were ordered to operate against the British. French shipping – of less importance both to France and to the German war-effort – remained inviolate.

With the mask off, Langsdorff considered his position, helped by appreciations from Berlin and his *B-Dienst* specialists on board. He was aware that, on the 2nd October a Pan-American Neutrality Zone would be declared by the American government, warning the European belligerents that no attacks on shipping within 300 miles of the coast of the Americas would be tolerated. He also knew that Mussolini's Italy would not, as she was bound to by treaty, come into the war at the side of her fellow Fascists, which meant that the British still had unrestricted access to the Suez Canal and the Mediterranean Sea. He also learned of the dispositions of the British Royal Navy.

The Royal Navy was not far away. Prior to the outbreak of war, during an increase in international tension between the European powers, the Royal Navy had mobilized. As noted the Home Fleet was on a war footing prior to 3 September and, during extensive exercises in August, the Reserve Fleet had also been mobilized. Immediately on the outbreak of war, in addition to instituting convoy for all merchant ships on the home coasts and Western Approaches, the British declared a blockade of Germany. Its first acts were to intercept

---

### HMSs *AJAX* and *ACHILLES*

Both were light cruisers of the *Leander*-class, a batch of five warships built between 1931 and 1934. They were followed by three 'improved' *Leander*s, the former being distinguished by their good looks and single funnel – the result of combining two boiler exhausts and ducting them together. The three later *Leander*s were all transferred to the Royal Australian Navy.

HMS *Ajax* was laid down at Vickers' shipyard at Barrow-in-Furness on 7 February 1933. Launched on 1 March 1934 she was commissioned on 3 June 1935. She was 169 metres in length overall, with a beam of 16.9 metres and a loaded draught of 5.8 metres. Her light displacement was 7,220 tons, 9,140 loaded.

Propulsion was by four Parsons geared steam turbines, supplied by six Admiralty three-drum boilers driving four screws. This generated 72,000shp (54 megawatts) and gave a top speed of 32.5 knots. Manned by a war establishment of 680 officers and ratings, she had a range of 32,000 nautical miles at a cruising speed of 15 knots.

With a main armament of eight 6-inch (152mm) guns in four turrets (A and B forward, X and Y aft), *Ajax* was a 'light' cruiser, designed for distant patrol work, battle fleet support, commerce protection and showing the flag, hence her ability to accommodate a flag officer.

---

homeward-bound German merchantmen, hence Nicholson's capture of the *Hannah Boge* off Iceland and Forbes's unsuccessful sweep in search of the Nord-Deutscher Lloyd liner *Bremen*, which was already safe in Murmansk and from there by way of neutral Norwegian waters reached the Fatherland. Despite errors, such as that of the British submarine *Triton* sinking the British submarine *Oxley*, the blockade was effective, if only in that German ships preferred to scuttle themselves to avoid capture. Most notably, however, the liner *Cap Norte*, 'which was carrying reservists from South America to Germany was successfully seized', but not until 9 October (she

In addition to her main armament she carried in 1939 a secondary armament of four 4-inch (102mm) guns, and an additional anti-aircraft battery of four 4-pounders. These were later increased in both cases to eight gun mountings. In addition she bore eight 21-inch (533mm) torpedo tubes in two broadside firing quadruple tubes sited amidships. For aerial reconnaissance in 1939 she carried a catapult-launched Fairey Seafox seaplane.

The class bore an armoured belt of 4-inch-thick steel tapering to 2-inch, with 2-inch armour on deck and 1-inch on the gun houses (turrets) and conning tower.

Substantially similar to her sister-ship *Ajax*, *Achilles* was laid down at Cammell Laird's Birkenhead yard on 11 June 1931 and launched into the River Mersey on 1 September 1932. She was commissioned on 6 October 1933 with a complement of 550 officers and ratings. This rose to 680 in time of war. She was transferred to the New Zealand Division on 31 March 1937, receiving a draft of New Zealanders who made up about 60 per cent of her crew. Key posts were retained by Britons until, in September 1941, the New Zealand Division of the Royal Navy became the Royal New Zealand Navy with its base at Devonport, Auckland. It was here that one of her gun turrets was mounted following her long service with the Indian Navy as INS *Delhi*, which lasted until June 1978.

afterwards became the troopship *Empire Trooper*). Farther afield, off the Rio de la Plata and in the first two days of the war, the British cruiser *Ajax*, flying the broad pendant of Commodore Henry Harwood, intercepted the German freighters *Carl Fritzen* and the *Olinda*. Off the West African coast the *Neptune* caught the *Inn*. Neither Harwood nor Vice Admiral D'Oyly Lyon, the Commander-in-Chief, South Atlantic, nor their masters in the Admiralty in London had an inkling that a powerful German raider lay in the offing between.

Langsdorff, on the other hand, thanks to *B-Dienst* intercepts, knew of both cruisers; and besides the *Neptune*, off West Africa, there were her fellow cruisers *Danae* and *Capetown* and the large submarine *Clyde*. Moreover, disposed along the eastern coast of South America with *Ajax*, was another submarine, the *Severn*, along with the destroyers *Havoc* and *Hotspur*, and HM Cruisers *Exeter*, *Cumberland*, *Achilles* and *Despatch* except that *Achilles*, though having a British captain, was His Majesty's New Zealand Ship (HMNZS). Langsdorff determined therefore to strike first at South American trade off Cabo São Roque where the shipping lanes converged on the shoulder of Brazil before swiftly withdrawing eastwards to lie in wait on the Cape route between the sea mounts of Ascension and St Helena. Leaving Dau in the waiting area, Langsdorff headed the *Admiral Graf Spee* towards Cabo São Roque intending to turn south off that headland and sweep down the coast and attack 'at the first opportunity'.

HMS *Exeter*

# 5 August–29 September: 'The Curtain Lifts'

As he headed north-west Raeder sent him another signal warning him to avoid engagement with enemy naval forces but paradoxically urging Langsdorff to attack mercantile shipping 'to the fullest extent'. Oddly, as Eric Grove points out, restrictions to Langsdorff's operational options were not only conditioned by Raeder's anxieties, but by more practical anxieties. The *Admiral Graf Spee*'s diesel engines were clocking up the running-hours, increasing potential break-down frequency, while her warm latitude 'required the refrigeration plant to keep the ammunition cool [. . .] Defects in the system also prevented her from operating north of 5° S[outh]'.

Notwithstanding these concerns, as his ship hastened to intercept a hapless merchantman or two, her company prepared the first of Langsdorff's deceptions: they converted the *Admiral Graf Spee* into the *Admiral Scheer*. This was easy enough: a change of nameplate on her quarterdeck, a few fake modifications about her upperworks and antennae. And thus disguised Langsdorff finally took the *Admiral Graf Spee* to war.

## 30 September–9 October: 'We Are, You See, at War'
On the afternoon of 30 September, as she approached Cabo São Roque, lookouts aboard the *Admiral Graf Spee* sighted smoke. Altering course to intercept but to keep his ship's silhouette 'end-on', and thus not reveal a characteristic profile well-known to British mariners since her appearance at the Coronation Review, Langsdorff went to action stations. Anxious that his quarry did not escape, he also catapulted his Arado floatplane; this could strafe the bridge of the targeted ship if she turned out to be British.

Proceeding upon her lawful occasions the 5,051-ton cargo liner *Clement*, engaged on the Booth Line's scheduled New York to Brazil service had departed from Pernambuco the previous day and was on the last leg of her outward passage which would terminate at Bahia. She was laden with a general cargo which included a large amount of paraffin and petrol (kerosene and gasoline) and steaming southwards at her service speed of 12.5 knots. Having just fixed the ship's latitude the *Clement*'s master, Captain F.C.P. Harris had gone below but was recalled to the bridge by her third mate who had seen the grey upperworks of a warship. Langsdorff's approaching tactic worked perfectly. Not only did Harris believe her to be British, 'probably HMS *Ajax*, as I had been aboard her a few weeks before in Pará and expected her to be about . . .' but he was deceived:

> I went up on the bridge and had a look at her with the glass, but as she was dead end-on to us I could make nothing out about her except that by the huge bow waves she was apparently closing us at great speed.

Anticipating the customary exchange of courtesies between the two services, Harris ensured the *Clement*'s red ensign streamed jauntily from its staff. He then went below to his cabin to 'put on a clean white uniform jacket'. As he returned to the bridge his illusions were shattered by the low pass made overhead by a seaplane: it bore the unmistakable black cross of Nazi Germany. The Arado's pilot, *Oberleutnant* Bongard, a *Luftwaffe* officer on secondment, having established the nationality of the vessel passing below him, banked steeply, turned and opened fire on the steamer's bridge. Whether this was against Langsdorff's orders, or in obedience to them is a matter of conjecture, but Harris knew where his duty lay: ordering the engines stopped and his radio officer to begin immediately transmitting the RRR signal that prefixed the *Clement*'s position and her identifying 'numbers', alerting all who were listening on the 500kHz distress frequency that they were a British merchantman under attack by a surface raider. He also ordered Chief Officer Jones to muster all hands on deck and swing the boats out.

> Three or four times more the 'plane passed over us, spraying the boat-deck and bridge with bullets, although the ship was stopped. The bullets fell around me on the bridge and around the men on the boat deck like hail. I can't understand [. . .] why some of us were not killed.

Approaching at speed, Langsdorff meanwhile was flashing a Morse signal ordering the *Clement* to heave-to; he followed this with a shell dropped ahead of the British vessel, which seems to have gone unobserved. Harris and his officers destroyed the confidential books and then, after doing everything necessary about the bridge, he

> went down on to the boat-deck where I found that everything was going along in true boat-drill fashion and that nearly all the boats were in the water. The only person wounded [. . .] was the Chief Officer, and he had blood on his right hand and forearm where two bullets had struck him.

By this time the *Admiral Graf Spee* had rounded-to about half a mile on the SS *Clement*'s port beam. Harris 'gave order to abandon ship. When we were all in the boats a piquet boat bore down on us and took the Chief Engineer and myself on board . . .'

**SS *Clement***

The two vessels wallowed, stopped in a low Atlantic swell, the black-funnelled liner lying under the trained guns of the commerce raider. Although orders had been received on the 24 September that granted permission to open fire on merchant ships when they transmitted wireless warnings that they were under attack, Langsdorff had not used his guns, nor did he have the signal jammed. Having embarked Harris and his chief engineer, Mr W. Bryant, Langsdorff allowed the *Clement*'s chief officer, Mr Jones, to pull the lifeboats clear of the ship. On passing under the *Panzerschiff*'s stern,

Harris and Bryant had observed 'the embossed letters on her quarter, *Admiral Scheer*, which, of course, had been painted over with grey'. Some trouble had clearly been gone to in this cunning double bluff, which deceived both Britons. When brought before him Langsdorff saluted Harris, shook his hand and then smiled, apologizing to Harris in English. 'I am sorry, Captain, but I have to sink your ship. We are, you see, at war.'

This courteous flurry done, Langsdorff ordered two torpedoes fired to sink his victim. Both missed, either passing ahead and astern of their target, or suffering from pistol-failure. It was something of a humiliation and worse was to come for the gunnery officer, Paul Ascher. Ordering the secondary armament of 15cm guns to open fire, twenty-five rounds were shot at the *Clement* but the rolling of the *Admiral Graf Spee* prevented an effective hole being made at the waterline (though Harris said 'there was practically no swell'). Nor was any of the *Clement*'s inflammable cargo ignited. Faced with this stubborn refusal to sink, Langsdorff ordered the main armament trained on her and five 28cm shells were fired at point-blank range. Built by Cammell-Laird at Birkenhead only five years previously she was, as Harris – who had been sunk in the First World War and appeared to the Germans as an elderly man – growled while watching this act of vandalism, 'a damned tough ship'.

The *Admiral Graf Spee*'s Artillery Technical Officer, F.W. Rasenack, admitted Harris 'had done good work. He had destroyed all the documents, plans, wireless apparatus and the principal engines [. . .] so, as we cannot take her to a neutral port, we must sink her . . .'

In the end she succumbed at 16.40, five and a half hours after the first sighting. But it was not a good start. Apart from the failure of the torpedoes and gunnery to despatch swiftly an unresisting British merchantman, the expenditure of ammunition had been excessive. This worried Rasenack, despite this first sinking being 'like a drop of Vermouth'. Nevertheless, Langsdorff watched as the cluster of lifeboats drew together and then called out to them through a megaphone the course necessary to reach the Brazilian coast. It was unnecessarily gratuitous advice; the *Clement*'s officers were regulars on the coast, more so than the Germans. Langsdorff also alerted the coast radio station Olinda at Pernambuco to the presence of British survivors in lifeboats, requesting the transmission of an 'All ships' (CQ) signal for assistance. Rasenack reported a ship being seen coming to the assistance of Jones and his boats. Thus was the foundation stone of Langsdorff's compassion laid, despite the zeal of his Arado aircrew. Yet it was ultimately self-serving, for he signed the message '*Admiral Scheer*': not an opportunity was to be lost to fox the enemy.

The *Clement*'s boats were then left heading west as the *Admiral Graf Spee* sped away southward. Some of the survivors were picked up by the Brazilian steamer *Itatinga* and landed at Maceió on 1 October, the rest made it ashore next day. Harris and his chief engineer were released within hours, too dangerous to retain on board for fear they might discover the true name of the German ship and too useful as decoys to imprison. 'About five hours' after departing from the scene of devastation, Langsdorff stopped the Greek steamship *Papalemos* for examination. Finding none of her cargo was consigned to Great Britain he extracted a promise that the Greek master would not make any radio transmission until he reached the Azores. He put Harris and his colleague on board knowing that, in due course, the report that the *Clement* had been sunk would reach London. That this consisted of false intelligence only added piquancy to Langsdorff's success, mitigating a little the practical difficulties, and, so Langsdorff hoped, causing confusion in the Admiralty.

In this Langsdorff succeeded. First intelligence reached London on Sunday 1 October, but details were sketchy. Both the British cable ship *Norseman* and the liner *Almanzora* had intercepted a garbled version of the raider-warning. Survivors landed from the *Itatinga* at Maceió reported the enemy ship's name as that of the *Admiral Scheer*. Harris corroborated this when he and Bryant were landed at São Vicente but by then the fat was in the fire. That the *Admiral Scheer*, attacked by RAF Blenheims in the Schillig Roads on the 5 September, had escaped to attack shipping in the South Atlantic was remarkable enough, but it raised another question: where on earth – quite literally – were the *Deutschland* and the *Admiral Graf Spee*?

# The Battle of the River Plate

The answer came in part on 5 October when the *Deutschland* sank the 5,000-ton British tramp *Stonegate* 500 miles east of Bermuda. On this same day Langsdorff, now off Ascension, 2,000 miles to the east of his first hit, encountered the British tramp *Newton Beech*. On his passage Langsdorff had sought to compound his deception by disguising his ship still further, repainting the foremast to look like a tripod structure and, again approaching his quarry end-on, he fooled the officer-of-the-watch aboard the heavily laden Newcastle-registered tramp ship as she made her laborious way to join a convoy at Freetown. Owned by the Tyneside Line of Ridley and Tully, she had been built by Pickersgill in 1925 and bore in her capacious holds some 7,600 tons of maize.

Nor was Captain Robison much the wiser until Langsdorff's radioed threats and elevating guns compelled him to stop the *Newton Beech*. 'You are damned early,' Robison is reported to have said on meeting the boarding party. He had taken the warship for a French man-of-war. Although a wireless message had been transmitted, the radio was being run on accumulators, not power from the ship's mains. The ingrained tight-fistedness that arose in part from the Depression years and in part from the endemic parsimony of certain ship owners, seems to have prevented the running of the ship's generators. Moreover, not only was the signal weak, it seems that it may have been a standard SOS, not the RRR signal, which might have alerted the recipient to the unwelcome presence of a hostile commerce raider. This recipient was another merchantman which, in conformity with international procedure, passed it on by Aldis-lamp to a passing British warship. Alas, its content was not recognized for what it truly was by the captain of HMS *Cumberland*, nor was it passed on to Vice Admiral D'Oyly Lyon, the Commander-in-Chief, South Atlantic, based at Freetown, whose staff might have put two-and-two together. Consequently Lyon remained ignorant of the *Admiral Graf Spee*'s presence within his bailiwick. Indeed, the SOS signal which ought to have sparked off a search in any case, seems not to have been taken seriously by anyone.

This lapse seemed to have marked a change in Langsdorff's luck, for the *Newton Beech*'s officers did not react quickly enough to their situation; the German boarding party rapidly overran the bridge and engine room, saving the ship, her contents and her confidential books. Invaluable to Langsdorff in his quest for enemy shipping were the Admiralty's general routeing instructions to all British masters. He now possessed the knowledge of where the naval staff in Whitehall advised British merchantmen to proceed to avoid the enemy. 'A most valuable find for us,' wrote Rasenack later.

SS *Newton Beech*

Having withdrawn Robison for instructions, Langsdorff sent him back to his ship and manned the *Newton Beech* with a well-armed prize crew. Thus coerced and intimidated, Robison and his crew were obliged to conform to the German warship's movements as a *Lumpensammler*, a supply source for her captor. So, with the laden tramp following at 9 knots, Langsdorff headed eastwards towards another rendezvous with Dau, whom he summoned from the *Altmark*'s waiting position to a point off Ascension. Meanwhile he looted the *Newton Beech* of anything useful that might extend his stores and thus the *Admiral Graf Spee*'s operational longevity.

But Wennecker and Langsdorff were not the only ones bestirring themselves on 5 October. Energized by the newly recalled and vigorous First Lord of the Admiralty, Winston Churchill, who had immediately contacted the French Ministry of the Marine along with Admiral Sir Dudley Pound, the First Sea Lord, eight British and

# The Battle of the River Plate

French squadrons were organized to hunt down the mysterious raider at large in the South Atlantic. The disposition of these assets indicates not only the extent of the combined sea power of the two Allies, but the inevitability of the eventual location of the German ship. In the far north, off Brest, Force L was made up by the French battleship *Dunkerque*, the carrier *Béarn*, and the cruisers *Georges Leygues*, *Gloire* and *Montcalm*. Across the North Atlantic and operating in the general area of North America and the West Indies, Force F consisted of the heavy cruisers HMSs *Berwick* and *York*. In the West Indies itself Force N was a combined squadron made up of the French battleship *Strasbourg* with the British carrier *Hermes* and cruiser *Neptune*. As far away as Ceylon (modern Sri Lanka) Force I covered the Indian Ocean and consisted of the aircraft carrier *Eagle* and the cruisers HMSs *Dorsetshire* and *Cornwall*.

In the wake of the raider's first appearance off Pernambuco, Force K had been assembled: the aircraft carrier HMS *Ark Royal* and the battlecruiser HMS *Renown*. Off Dakar, on the other side of the Atlantic Narrows, lay Force M; this French squadron was made up from the cruisers *Dupleix* and *Foch*, while convoy escort forces at the neighbouring British rendezvous of Freetown had been reinforced by the seaplane carrier *Albatross*, able to carry out aerial reconnaissance. Off Cape Town, HM Cruisers *Shropshire* and *Sussex* formed Force H.

And finally – and ultimately fatally to Langsdorff and his ship – off the east coast of South America was Harwood's cruiser squadron, Force G, then made up of *Cumberland* and *Exeter*. In reserve were the *Ajax* and *Achilles*, then in the Falklands, Harwood's base being Port Stanley, like that of Sturdee, Graf von Spee's nemesis a generation earlier. Forces G, H and K were under the overall command of D'Oyly Lyon at Freetown and they were committed to 'long and anxious searches in the wastes of the South Atlantic'. Although this vast net was cast wide, within it Langsdorff was by no means yet enmeshed. Indeed his run of luck continued for, with the *Newton Beech* trailing in the offing, he was to run directly into his next victim at 08.30 on 7 October.

She was another Tyneside tramp, the *Ashlea*, 4,222 gross registered tons and owned by the Cliffside Shipping Co Ltd of John Morrison and Son. She was down to her marks, carrying 7,300 tons of sugar, on passage from Capetown to Britain and had a crew of thirty-four, eight of whom were West Africans. Captain Charles Pottinger was also taken by surprise, perhaps thinking the stranger a French cruiser. He was in no doubts when a large board was raised which bore the words: DO NOT USE WIRELESS. STOP ENGINES. IF YOU DISOBEY – WE FIRE. Running below to his cabin Pottinger managed to destroy his papers as the warship's lowered motor boats approached at speed. It was all he could do for, at this stage of the war and outside the so-called war zones in which convoy was compulsory, ships like the *Ashlea* carried insufficient radio officers to maintain a twenty-four hour watch. Although the *Ashlea*'s radio officer is thought to have made a transmission on his own initiative, no warning signal seems to have been picked up by either the *B-Dienst* operators scrupulously monitoring the airwaves for any infringement of Langsdorff's warning, or a friendly operator elsewhere, before the booted and armed boarding party ascended the laden ship's low freeboard and clambered aboard.

SS *Ashlea*

Rasenack failed to recognize the *Ashlea* as a tramp ship, taking her for a cargo liner. She was, he wrote, 'very different from the *Newton Beech* – which like all tramps is a dirty ship – [and] makes an excellent impression. The officers wear white uniforms, the captain is

a gentleman in every sense of the word and replies to us courteously
. . .'

Taking the mate's logbook, a quantity of sugar and some potatoes, the German sailors transferred the *Ashlea*'s crew to the wretched *Newton Beech* now making a smoky appearance over the horizon and, to be certain of swift demolition and chary of wasting ammunition, set charges in the ship's engine room. It was dark when she blew up; a few of her hands watched forlornly from the rail of the German warship.

Having disposed of the *Ashlea* Langsdorff now determined to rid himself of his earlier prize. Unable to remove anything further useful from the *Newton Beech* and frustrated by the low speed of the British steamer, not helped by poor-quality coal, Langsdorff withdrew all prisoners that evening into hurriedly prepared accommodation aboard the *Admiral Graf Spee*. He then scuttled the *Newton Beech* with explosive charges, after which he arranged another rendezvous with the *Altmark*.

Dau, meanwhile, had had a lucky escape. Like his senior officer, Heinrich Dau had also disguised his ship, choosing the distinctive funnel of the American Delta Line of New Orleans and having the name *Delmar* painted on the *Altmark*'s bow. She had already masqueraded as the *Sogne* of Oslo and, in addition to that first alarum, had dodged what might have been an enemy, or at least a pair of eyes to see her and a brain minded to play the informer. With her four MAN-diesels, the 11,000-ton *Altmark* was capable of 21 knots and could outrun most casual observers on the high seas, but on 9 October Dau's lookouts spotted an aircraft approaching. Aerial reconnaissance in such a remote location meant only one thing – the proximity of an aircraft carrier. With the ship lying stopped, Dau could do nothing but play at being who he was pretending, despite the fact that the *Altmark* was not making way – most unusual for a merchantman unless she was broken down – and her crew 'were seen to be sunbathing and fishing over the side'. This inactivity did not strike Captain A. J. Power of HMS *Ark Royal* odd at the time, for he attributed his aircrew's failure 'to penetrate her disguise' to their being 'inexperienced in those days'. The plane flew off, returning to

*Ark Royal*, then on her way from Brazil towards Freetown but still in search of the putative *Admiral Scheer*. The observer's report raised sufficient doubt in the minds of Captain Power and Rear Admiral L.V. Wells, who ordered a second air patrol to further verify the identity of the reported tanker. Ship recognition information suggested that the *Delmar* was a freighter.

Once again, fortune favoured the Germans; it was already twilight by the time the *Ark Royal's* second aircraft reached the last reported position of the '*Delmar*'. There was, of course, no sign of her in the gathering darkness. Only later did Wells discover that the real *Delmar* was then in New Orleans.

The *B-Dienst* Service (or to give it its full name the *Funkbeobachtungsdienst*) provided Langsdorff with high-quality communications and intelligence-gathering input. The operators were civilians working for the *Kriegsmarine*'s Intelligence Division sent to sea on secondment. The service's specialist *xB-Dienst* section had begun to break British naval codes as early as 1936 and by 1939 Berlin had little trouble reading the British Admiralty's operational signals or of passing intelligence culled thus to its operational chiefs or units afloat or ashore. They knew besides the British Merchant Ship Code. Such codes were hand-generated and not mechanized and it was Wilhelm Tranow who was chiefly responsible for this breakthrough. Although the British attempted to limit all radio traffic, the sheer volume of naval movements and mass of merchant shipping meant that the enemy derived a great deal of useful intelligence from intercepts.

## 10–21 October: 'A Serious Strain . . .'

Langsdorff's own aerial eyes were blind on 10 October; the Arado underwent an engine-change, for the seaplane's nose suffered from being doused with sea water on landing and the cylinder block had cracked. This circumstance did not prevent the *Admiral Graf Spee*'s lookouts, equipped with excellent Zeiss binoculars, from spotting the tall funnel and masts of the cargo liner *Huntsman*.

# The Battle of the River Plate

Owned by T. and J. Harrison's Charente Steamship Company of Liverpool, the *Huntsman* was a 12-knot steam turbine cargo liner of 8,196 tons. She was operating in a joint service with Cayzer Irvine's Clan Line and on her way home from Calcutta with a mixed and valuable cargo of 11,000 tons of carpets, jute, tea (sufficient 'to supply the whole of England for forty-five days', according to Rasenack), mineral ore and gum. Having some space remaining after she left the Hughli, she had called at Colombo and then headed across the Arabian Sea for the Strait of Bab-el-Mandeb. After lifting more cargo in Port Sudan, she had headed up the Red Sea for the Suez Canal. Shortly afterwards she was intercepted by a British cruiser which, anticipating Italy's entry into the war, had informed Captain A. Brown that the canal was closed pending developments. Under the powers invoked by the Naval Control of Shipping Act, Brown was ordered to Aden and from thence to Mombasa and Durban. Here he received orders from Harrisons to proceed to Freetown for onward convoy. This was a frustration: Brown was sixty-three years old, on his last voyage before retirement and the prolongation of his voyage would have to be endured.

*SS Huntsman*

# 10-21 October: 'A Serious Strain . . .'

By the early evening of the 10th, the *Huntsman* had doubled the Cape of Good Hope and was well on her way up the South Atlantic, standing towards the Equator in a position of Latitude 8° 30' South, Longitude 005° 15' West. The majority of her crew, fifteen British officers and engineers and sixty-seven Indian lascars, had gone to dinner as it grew dark – about 19.00 ship's time – when the silhouette of an approaching warship was sighted to the east. As she drew close Brown and his officer-of-the-watch, studying the stranger, found some relief in the fact that they could discern the French tricolour.

But even as he watched, the French ensign was lowered and in its place the *Swastika*-emblazoned German ensign was run up, and with it came the peremptory signal: 'Stop!' As Brown reached for the engine room telegraph, he passed word to the radio officer, B.C. McCorry, to get off a raider-warning transmission. Brown himself had no time to destroy his confidential papers as Langsdorff warned that if the wireless transmission continued, he would open fire. Brown bowed to the inevitable.

Meanwhile, at least according to Rasenack: 'On deck there are sixty-seven Hindus running about, completely panicked. They fear for their lives.' McCorry, on the other hand, afterwards asserted the Indian crew, 'proved entirely loyal to Britain and impervious to attempts to turn them against the British'. Such calumnies were common among the Germans, who failed to comprehend the complex inter-racial ties that entangled men sharing their lives aboard British merchantmen.

An officer and armed boarding party were shortly afterwards on board and Brown and Mr A.H. Thompson, his chief officer, were removed to the *Admiral Graf Spee*. As had occurred to the *Newton Beech*, the two men were allowed back to their ship with strict instructions to conform with Langsdorff's movements and ordered to proceed to a rendezvous position. Back on board the *Huntsman*, Brown was given a certificate by way of receipt for his surrendered ship by the German officer commanding the prize.

Meanwhile, believing McCorry's signal must have been intercepted, Langsdorff transmitted to Berlin a fast-flash signal of his strikes, their cumulative tonnage and other intelligence gleaned from his captures. Among this was new information about British codes yielded by the *Huntsman*'s papers. Langsdorff also ordered a quick transmission on the *Huntsman*'s radio that her attacker had been a submarine, intending to confuse his enemy; unfortunately his enemy failed to pick up any of the three signals and remained ignorant of events in their midst, even as they themselves guilelessly informed the *B-Dienst* men of their own scattered movements.

To this serendipitous intelligence, Langsdorff was now able to learn from the *Huntsman*'s documents that instead of sending lone cruisers to patrol along the trade routes, which had been the method of trade protection thought adequate in the first years of the First World War and which was one way of covering the sea lanes outside the umbrella of convoy in the Second, the Allied naval dispositions were concentrating at the focal choke-points: off West Africa, off Cabo São Roque, Gibraltar, the Cape of Good Hope and the Rio de la Plata. Next day, Thursday, 12 October, he learned that the *Ajax* was back on the Brazilian coast, having been refuelling at Rio de Janeiro. It was now time for another rendezvous with Dau.

The Allies' search for German commerce raiders was bearing little fruit. It was true that on 16 October the French cruiser *Duguay Trouin* had forced the Hamburg-Amerika Linie's *Halle* to scuttle herself when intercepted west of Dakar. But against this had to be set, not only Langsdorff's successes, but those of his colleague Wennecker, operating far to the north, paltry though they were. On the 9th, the *Deutschland* had captured the American freighter the *City of Flint*, one of the vessels that had rescued survivors from the sinking *Athenia* on the very first day of the war. She was to prove a nuisance, being taken into neutral Norwegian waters by her prize crew from where, following furious protests from Washington, she had, perforce, to be released. But on the 14th, Wennecker had sunk the Norwegian freighter *Lorentz W. Hansen*. Despite the claim that she carried contraband and that Wennecker had left her crew in their lifeboats to fend for themselves, ironically the complications of a German attack on a neutral ship had worse repercussions for the British in terms of international relations than for the Germans. All this was scant consolation to a frustrated Churchill and First Sea Lord Admiral Sir

Dudley Pound in the Admiralty, who remained largely in the dark as to the true picture of enemy dispositions in both the North, but particularly the South Atlantic. They had endured a further alarm on 8 October when the *Gneisenau*, *Köln* and a destroyer flotilla had sortied into the North Sea and along the Norwegian coast. Forbes had left Scapa with the Home Fleet and then, when it was learned that the German squadron was back in the Schillig Roads, taken the bulk of his ships to anchor in Loch Ewe. Thus, on the 14th, the *Royal Oak* was the only capital ship in Scapa Flow when Günther Prien penetrated the defences in *U-47* and sank her. This was a bad blow for British prestige, as much as alarming for those responsible for the security of the Home Fleet's anchorage. By this time, however, Churchill and Pound had confirmation from the masters of the *Clement* and the *Stonegate*, both now released, that at least two pocket battleships were at large. Which these were, remained uncertain.

Hitler himself was now worried about the fate of the two *Panzerschiffs*, especially that of the *Deutschland*, whose loss would, he felt, deal a serious blow to morale. Accordingly Wennecker was ordered home, covered by a second sortie by the *Gneisenau*, this time with her sister-ship *Scharnhorst* in company. On 23 November they fell upon the Armed Merchant Cruiser HMS *Rawalpindi*, in happier times a P & O liner, but then engaged in the Northern Blockade, patrolling between Iceland and the Faeroes. Shortly after destroying her, the two German capital ships turned for home, their mission to cover Wennecker's retreat completed. Having passed through the Denmark Strait on the 9th, then reached the Norwegian coast, Wennecker turned the *Deutschland* south, doubled the Naze of Norway, passed through the Skagerrak, the Kattegat and the Øresund. Finally, on 15 November, Wennecker berthed the *Deutschland* in Gotenhafen, as the German-occupied Polish port of Gdynia was now called.

With his sensitively named ship back in port, the Führer ordered her rechristened the *Lützow*. But if her cruise had been a failure, not merely by the paucity of ships sunk, the diplomatic crisis with Oslo and, more importantly, Washington, had succeeded in foxing the opposition. Forbes had had the two hunting groups Forces H and K, destined for the South Atlantic, diverted back to the north in quest of the *Deutschland*, a situation that remained unchanged until mid-December, when all became clear. The material dividends had consisted of one blockade-runner: one of *Ark Royal*'s aircraft had spotted the Hansa Line's *Uhenfels*, and the escorting destroyer *Hereward* had been despatched to capture her on 5 November. Taken into Freetown, she was no mean prize, for in addition to her general cargo of hides, nuts and copra, she yielded a consignment of opium worth £250,000. Notwithstanding this, the debit was greater. 'The mere presence of this powerful ship upon our main trade route,' Churchill afterwards wrote of the *Deutschland*, 'had imposed [. . .] as was intended, a serious strain upon our [convoy] escorts and hunting groups on the North Atlantic.'

Thus the dominant place occupied in the collective thinking of the British Admiralty posed by surface commerce raiders and their potential to further damage British merchant shipping led to more counter-measures. On 15 October the Admiralty had requisitioned three new and fast 18-knot cargo liners owned by Alfred Holt & Co's Glen Line. One, the *Glenearn*, having been taken over on the outbreak of war by the Ministry of Shipping and turned into a military transport, had already made three voyages to Brest carrying tanks and military vehicles. On 22 October she arrived at Palmer's Tyneside yard at Hebburn for conversion to a fleet supply ship designed to keep supplied at sea the squadrons hunting for the elusive raiders of the *Kriegsmarine*.

Meanwhile, on that same 15 October the British Admiralty had taken measures to supply their own warships, the *Admiral Graf Spee* had refuelled and replenished from the *Altmark*. On his approach Langsdorff had the *Reichskriegsflagge* flying superior to four British red ensigns, evidence to the watching Dau and his officers, of the *Admiral Graf Spee*'s recent triumphs. Boarding her, Dau offered his congratulations, only to find Langsdorff with other things on his mind, preoccupied by the numbers of prisoners he had on board. This was a situation that could only worsen as his cruise lengthened, with a consequent long-term possibility of compromising his ship's efficiency. The solution, he explained to Dau, would be to accommodate them aboard the *Altmark*, though he would retain the masters, chief mates, chief engineers and radio officers aboard the *Admiral Graf Spee*. Notwithstanding this, Dau was unwilling to play gaoler to the majority and 'had an abiding hatred of the British dating back to his own captivity in Britain during the First World War'. He was also concerned that his own crew of 134 was inferior to the number of prisoners Langsdorff was contemplating placing aboard the *Altmark*. Langsdorff countered this objection by passing orders to supply a ten-man guard and an officer from the *Admiral Graf Spee*'s complement; the latter, *Leutnant zur See* Otto Schmidt, was to be personally responsible to Langsdorff for the security of the prisoners aboard Dau's ship.

Constructed for special service the *Altmark* had 'tween deck spaces intended for the stowage of supplies forward and aft of her oil-cargo tanks. Much of these had been emptied in resupplying the *Admiral Graf Spee* and some rationalization could take place, freeing up capacity. The forward spaces, immediately abaft her chain locker, would be cleared out and used for the bulk of the prisoners. This consisted of four 'flats' sealed off by cofferdams fore and aft. The after cofferdam was supplied with an elevating cage for the lifting of supplies to the deck above. These could be utilized, with some fruitful improvisation undertaken by the prisoners. Empty oil drums would convert to primitive lavatories, empty stores boxes could be made into tables and the crew of the *Huntsman* would be ordered to bring out of their ship jute and carpets for bedding and partitions. It was all very thorough, although a shortage of mugs was only solved by using empty canning tins. In this way provision was made for the mates and engineers to be accommodated in the upper flat, the next was to be fitted out as a wash-place and lavatory, with provision being made for upwards of a further hundred men in the two lowest spaces above the cellular double bottom tanks. The Indian lascars were to be segregated and placed in the limited space in the after section. Langsdorff gave Dau a couple of days to clear the spaces and restow his remaining stores and before they parted they celebrated the good news just then being broadcast from Berlin: Günther Prien had sunk the British battleship *Royal Oak* in a notable feat of arms.

At the second rendezvous on the 17th, in addition to the prisoners transferred from the *Admiral Graf Spee*, Dau was obliged to accept the crew of the *Huntsman*. Before leaving their ship their captors had ensured the *Huntsman*'s people raided the cargo and brought off the carpets and bales of jute required for their accommodation aboard the *Altmark*. They also looted 'white shoes, sun-helmets, leather [. . .] and many other things [. . .] We go on drawing treasures from her holds. Some 80 tons of goods are transferred to us from the *Altmark*. A real record at sea.'

The *B-Dienst* staff had also been busy and 'have managed to decypher the secret British code [. . .] and we will now be able to decypher the wireless messages between British merchantmen and the British Admiralty'.

The three vessels lay rolling easily as the transfer proceeded by motor boat and the sun was setting by the time all had been accomplished. Only one task remained, the sinking of the *Huntsman* and Dau manoeuvred the *Altmark* for the splendid photo opportunity he rather maliciously considered this event to be. Once again difficulty was experienced.

'It was 6 p.m. when the *Spee* first went into action against the helpless British freighter,' observed Willi Frischauer, with his co-author Robert Jackson after the war:

> The sun set on the horizon, the evening mists were settling on the sea when, disappointed to the verge of dejection, the *Altmark*'s crew gave up all hope of witnessing the death of the *Hunstman*. By then it was too dark to take any pictures.
>
> By 9 p.m. the deck was empty [. . .] They woke up next morning to be told that the *Huntsman* had sunk at midnight.

During the day of wallowing idleness the German engineering staff aboard the *Panzerschiff* had laboured to overhaul their main diesel engines. Langsdorff, meanwhile, armed with intelligence from his captures, *B-Dienst* intercepts and an appreciation based on the known locations of Anglo-French forces sent from Berlin, considered his options. He knew that Raeder wished as much for *disruption* to the enemy as for more quantifiable material success, but he was conscious that this had little meaning to his men or, he suspected, to others in Berlin. On the other hand his ship was, for all Dau's efforts, beginning to suffer from her sea time. Despite the engineers' exertions the main propulsion would grow increasingly problematic, while the refrigerating plant was already giving cause for concern. Langsdorff calculated he would have to make his dash back to Germany passing through the dangerous northern waters during the dark, new moon phase of January 1940. On the positive side, it was clear from all his sources that the Cape route offered him the best chance of further prizes, with a bolt-hole in the Indian Ocean if needed. He accordingly laid a course towards Walvis Bay, and the *Admiral Graf Spee* left a discontented Dau and his even more unhappy prisoners – knocking up primitive facilities in the *Altmark*'s forward flats – in his wake.

## 22 October–1 December: 'Even at the Risk of Losing the Ship'

Shortly after midday on 22 October 1939 the 5,299-ton *Trevannion* was heading north-west, homeward-bound from Port Pirie in Australia laden with washed ore concentrates. The *Trevannion* was owned by The Hain Steamship Company, a tramping subsidiary of P & O. She could lift 9,130 tons dead weight and make 10.5 knots, a new, diesel-engined tramp built in 1937 by Lithgows of Port Glasgow and a fine prize for Langsdorff. She had left Liverpool the previous January, discharging her outward cargo in San Francisco before tramping in the Pacific. Eventually her master, Captain J.M. Edwards, had received orders to proceed to Port Pirie and it was here that the *Trevannion* had been lying when war broke out. Sailing was delayed while the crew painted the ship grey and, following orders from Britain, a stern-chase gun was fitted. That done, they had headed west, topping off their bunkers at Cape Town on the 17th before laying a course for home.

At about noon they had seen a warship approaching. Edwards had already heard of the loss of the *Clement* and was concerned about the presence of German raiders, but again the German ship approached end-on and then, as she slowed and swung round, the French tricolour was conspicuous and reassuring. However, the mask was cast aside with the imperative orders to 'Stop! Heave-to! Do not use W/T' and 'I am sending a boat,' all received by Second Mate W. Platten. Realizing he had been fooled, Captain Edwards stood in the doorway of the radio room and instructed the young radio officer, N.C. Martinson, to transmit the *Trevannion*'s position, her identifying four-letter code (known as her 'Numbers') along with the RRR Signal indicating an attack by an enemy raider.

The monitoring operators aboard the *Admiral Graf Spee* passed word to the bridge that the *Trevannion* was transmitting, consequently Langsdorff ordered his 20mm cannon to open fire from a range of 'about 100 yards away [. . .] and they swept her right the way along', Edwards wrote later.

As the shells struck the *Trevannion*, Martinson hesitated but Edwards ordered him to repeat the transmission and Martinson courageously continued. A second prolonged burst of fire shook the British tramp, one shell penetrating the radio room, while Platten called out that the enemy ship was still signalling them to stop. By this time Edwards had dumped his confidential books and, ringing his engines astern, blew three blasts on the whistle to indicate that he was complying with Langsdorff's instructions. Shortly afterwards a boarding party put off from the raider and Platten made to go below to throw the pilot ladder over the side, but the gunfire had shot away the bridge ladder and he fell, injuring one foot. Nevertheless the pilot ladder was tossed over and, a few minutes later, the armed German boarding party scrambled up its obliging rungs.

Conversationally, the boarding party informed Edwards that the *Trevannion* had been spotted from the Arado at dawn before relieving him of his sextant. Martinson, who had only ceased transmitting as the Germans boarded, was given a verbal roughing-up, but before long they had all been removed to the *Admiral Graf Spee* and the *Trevannion* was scuttled with explosive charges. Soon after this, the *Admiral Graf Spee* was ordered west to where, 600 miles away, the *Altmark* was waiting, having been moved to a revised rendezvous by Raeder. The *Kreigsmarine*'s Commander-in-Chief, aware of the extent of the Anglo-French hue-and-cry, was an anxious man. Thus, six days later, on 28 October, another rendezvous was made with the *Altmark* in Latitude 26° 37' South and Longitude 017° 49' West. Of *Trevannion*'s crew all but Edwards, Martinson, the chief officer, Mr W. Venables, and the chief engineer, Mr N. Doye, were put aboard Dau's ship.

**SS *Trevannion***

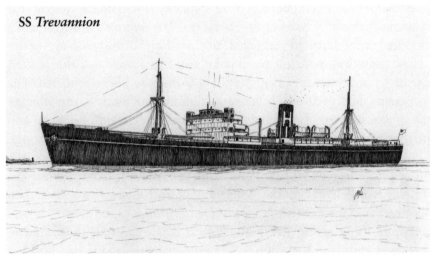

During the transfer of prisoners Dau, as was his habit, called upon Langsdorff and the two commanders concerted their movements. Langsdorff had to assume that the *Trevannion*'s prolonged transmissions had been intercepted, the reason why Raeder had shifted their present rendezvous so far west. It was clear too, that an interception of the *Trevannion*'s signals may well have compromised operations on the Cape route and that both for secrecy and to confuse the enemy a further dispersal should ensue. Raeder had advised Langsdorff to adopt this course of action, but its logic must have been equally clear to Langsdorff and his colleague. Accordingly, therefore, Dau was ordered south into the wastes of the Southern Ocean and well away from the trade routes that converged on the Cape. Langsdorff would head south too, but then stretch away to the eastwards before swinging north, doubling the Cape in a high latitude before striking again in the Indian Ocean. The two men agreed to meet again in a fortnight before saying their farewells.

# The Battle of the River Plate

Langsdorff and Raeder were correct; the *Trevannion*'s distress call had been intercepted by the radio officers aboard the Union-Castle liner *Llanstephan Castle* who, in turn, had relayed it to the Royal Naval station at Freetown. But the confusion in the Admiralty plotting room remained, for the intelligence did not quite add up. One problem arose from either an error in position arising from Martinson's original signal, or a mistake introduced during the relaying process. Whatever its cause, the *Trevannion*'s position when attacked was wrongly received in London. Unfortunately, in an almost identical position to that believed to have been that of the enemy's last attack on a British ship, a U-boat had been reported. The increasing bite of the U-boats thus clouded the picture, introducing the possibility of the signal being deliberate misinformation and further devaluing Martinson's gallantly made signal. Although London knew that a *Panzerschiff* had sunk the *Clement* and the *Stonegate*, this was still thought to be the *Admiral Scheer*, while the *Rawalpindi*, victim of the *Scharnhorst* and *Gneisenau*, was then assumed to have been sunk by the *Deutschland*.

The hunting groups, of which much was expected, continued to intercept only the occasional German merchantman, but nothing more substantial. Meanwhile Dau dodged to the southwards, sometimes under easy revolutions, sometimes at full speed, but confronting real anxiety when Langsdorff failed to show up for the intended rendezvous in mid-November.

*Grossadmiral* Raeder's advice that he could, if he wished, move his theatre of operations into the Indian Ocean on the grounds that such a move would certainly further confuse the British, was congruent with Langsdorff's own thoughts. On 30 October, on his way to strike east of the Cape of Good Hope, Langsdorff addressed his crew and told them that he would be heading home in the New Year, meanwhile Berlin had signalled he should award 100 Iron Crosses to deserving members of the ship's company. The news boosted morale, which was under some strain as the *Admiral Graf Spee* again demonstrated her poor sea-keeping qualities in the heavy seas of the Southern Ocean. For two days Langsdorff was obliged to heave-to but in those conditions his plan matured. He would loop east and then north, crossing the lonely rhumb-line between the Cape and Australia, and venture farther north, in the quieter waters to the south of Madagascar. After making his kill, this time as the *Admiral Graf Spee*, he would double back into the South Atlantic, where he would strike again at the Cape Route, masquerading as the *Admiral Scheer*.

On 9 November, in his new hunting area to the south of Cape St Mary, Madagascar, the sea conditions had moderated sufficiently to fly off the re-engined Arado. It saw nothing of the ships expected to be carrying the proceeds of the Australian shearing season and returned to land alongside, splashing down in a welter of water. When it was recovered by crane, cracks were discovered in the replacement engine-block: it was clear they had few flying hours left in the machine. Like the propulsion motors and the refrigeration plant they would be lucky to last out Langsdorff's planned sea time.

Langsdorff did not know that the Australian wool-clip had been delayed that year so he edged slowly west, havering a little. He considered sending the Arado on a final mission to bomb the oil tanks at Durban, but decided against it on the grounds that it would almost certainly lead to his being located. Better perhaps to move across the southern end of the wide strait between Madagascar and the Portuguese overseas territory of Mozambique. Again, he encountered nothing as he slowly closed the coast to the north of the Portuguese administrative capital of Lourenço Marques. In the darkness of the evening of 14 November his lookouts reported a vessel in the offing. She turned out to be a small, neutral Dutchman, and while Langsdorff considered boarding her, he dismissed the idea as too risky in the rough seas then running.

The *Admiral Graf Spee* was now almost courting disaster, coasting the shore hoping to trap an unwary merchant ship. It is a measure of Langsdorff's frustration that he took what might appear an almost foolhardy risk. But it was vital that, if his plan was to work, he must be *reported* in the Indian Ocean, irrespective of the actual damage he might thereby inflict. He was banking on his engineers' ability to maintain high speed long enough to drop any inquisitive eyes over the horizon astern of him after his display of force. The day following the tempting but impractical target of the Dutchman, lookouts reported a small tanker inshore of the *Admiral Graf Spee*. Langsdorff ordered an interception.

Whether or not the *Admiral Graf Spee* penetrated the neutral waters of Mozambique is a matter for conjecture. The master of the small coastal tanker *Africa Shell* (owned by the Anglo-Saxon Petroleum Company's east African subsidiary and running south in ballast to load another cargo of gasoline with which to keep supplied the flying boats that flew the length of Africa on behalf of British Imperial Airways) thought so. Captain Patrick Dove's brand-new but diminutive command – of which he was extremely proud – grossed a little over 700 tons, but the news of her sinking was relayed by the outraged Portuguese news service from Lourenço Marques, for she had been despatched off Inhambane and was close enough for Langsdorff to allow her crew to take to the boats and make for the coast. Only Captain Dove was retained aboard the *Admiral Graf Spee*.

**SS *Africa Shell***

The sinking of the *Africa Shell*, small though she was, was enough to satisfy Langsdorff's desire to show his undisguised hand in the Indian Ocean, though he was disappointed that she was empty and in ballast. News of the attack and of its victim – though less specifically of its perpetrator – would soon be known to the British and, sure enough, warning of an enemy commerce raider was transmitted to all ships from Durban next day. Shortly after the encounter, the German warship passed a Japanese merchantman, which she left alone, but made certain that she held her north-easterly course as long as the Japanese vessel remained in sight. Langsdorff then turned his ship south-east.

The next day, 16 November, Langsdorff stopped a Dutch cargo liner the *Mapia*, but allowed her to proceed towards Sumatra after extracting a promise from her master to maintain radio silence. Langsdorff continued on a south-easterly course until next day when he swung to the south-west. Notwithstanding his anxiety over his engines, he was sanguine that he would intercept more British ships on his way home. Having struck a well-publicized blow as the *Admiral Graf Spee*, Langsdorff doubled back round the Cape of Good Hope, again making a wide sweep south, well away from aerial reconnaissance or the shipping lanes off South Africa. Deep in the Southern Ocean the *Admiral Graf Spee* struggled through heavy weather, again displaying her lack of sea-kindliness; Captain Dove – who had served in sail in the four-masted barque *Olivebank* – afterwards wrote in a book of his experiences that to the 'young German crew, most of whose experience had been confined to the enclosed waters of the Baltic, heading into this mountainous sea was something too much for them. They could scarcely believe that a ship of ten thousand tons of steel could be buffeted and flung about like a plaything [. . .] She was pitching and rolling [. . .] and time after time she buried her foredeck in solid green seas right over her forward gun turret.'

By the 22nd the *Admiral Graf Spee* had doubled the Cape and was heading north-west into better weather, good enough for the crew to turn-to and begin to raise a dummy funnel, paint the Arado and rig a dummy third gun turret out of canvas and wood. The extent of this new disguise, and the nature of it, spawned those rumours common on board ship when the intentions of the commander are obscure. Was this odd conversion intended to deceive more British merchantmen, or was it meant to deceive the questing warships of the

The *Mapia*, a Dutch cargo liner.

Royal Navy in their hunt for the elusive *Panzerschiff*? And, if the latter, how close would they come before they blew their cover and opened fire?

The men worked with an enthusiastic will for six days. All hands knew of the critical state of the ship's engines; it was a racing certainty that they must go home and to do so run the British blockade. To this end they must make the *Admiral Graf Spee* as like a British battlecruiser as possible, hence the second funnel raised on the after gunnery-control position and a carefully added second turret forward, 'formed by our night director control tower and by the forward director control tower. On these two we have stretched painted cloth'. To this, erected on the lower bridge, the long pseudo-barrels were added, being supported by thin vertical 'toms', invisible at a distance to produce a silhouette which, at a distance, would approximate HMS *Renown*, by now well-known to be operating all over the Atlantic in search of the pocket battleship.

While undergoing this modification to her appearance, the *Panzerschiff* was idling in the waiting area, roughly equidistant from Walvis Bay, Tristan da Cunha and Rio de Janeiro, and with the power requirement reduced, the *Admiral Graf Spee*'s engineering department was once again employed carrying out a running overhaul. The main engines, unit by unit, had their piston rings changed, and the auxiliary plant was made good where possible. Overside on stages the seamen and other co-opted ratings not otherwise gainfully employed covered the topsides with a grey tone similar to that used by the British in the Atlantic theatre. The same paint was used to break up the *Admiral Graf Spee*'s upperworks to closer resemble the *Renown*.

While his engineers made the best of a bad job and an over-anxious Dau hurried towards him in the *Altmark*, Langsdorff came to a conclusion that sealed the fate of his ship and himself. According to Captain Dove, with whom Langsdorff seems to have struck up an acquaintanceship that extracted a curious candour from the German commander, Langsdorff admitted that he had some difficulty making his officers understand the special service the *Admiral Graf Spee* was on. Commerce-raiding, Langsdorff argued, was a 'particular kind of work'. 'Often,' he confessed, 'I have difficulty in explaining to my officers that I am not a coward.' His officers wanted a conventional naval engagement, wanted to measure their steel against that of the vaunted Royal Navy. In short they wanted another Coronel, though without the fatal sequence: annihilation off the Falklands.

Thus far – and whatever his officers thought – Langsdorff had acquitted his task well, but in the brief respite while he waited for his engine repairs to be completed and the *Altmark* to arrive, he had a change of heart. At noon on 24 November he summoned his officers and informed them that they would now be making their way back to Germany, though not without causing mayhem on the way. He then informed them of his volte-face: if they encountered British men-of-war they would not dodge away, but engage them 'even,' according to *Oberleutnant zur See* Rasenack, the second gunnery officer, 'at the risk of losing the ship'. This was an extraordinary decision for Langsdorff to make – and to make publicly – though it is easy with hindsight to see that privately he might have considered that in running the gauntlet north the length of the Atlantic Ocean, he would be exceedingly lucky not to have to fight his way home at one stage or another. Perhaps, given this probability, it was better to raise morale by appealing to the belligerent instincts of his young crew – men trained to fight and most of them imbued with the Nazi creed – than to let it happen with his ship's company psychologically unprepared.

During the long day of 26th, after the rendezvous had been made with *Altmark* – in position Latitude 25° South, Longitude 010° West – with the motor launches shuttling back and forth and the *Admiral Graf Spee* trailing slowly in the wake of the tanker, secured by a line and with an umbilical hose filling her diesel tanks, Langsdorff committed his reasons to paper. There can be little doubt that this was in self-justification – perhaps self-exculpation – for what he had proposed publicly was in contravention to his orders. Clearly at the heart of his thinking, and the need to deliberate the matter, was the state of his ship's main propulsion. After over 30,000 running hours it was increasingly unreliable. Marine diesel engines had been introduced into merchant ships for some time before the building of the *Panzerschiff*, but these were relatively low powered. What was required for the German warship was a sixfold increase on this standard norm. As the contemporary British shipping expert A.C. Hardy wrote in 1946, this was 'something which might have daunted the most imaginative and daring of naval constructors . . .' He went on to say:

> [H]owever, the German Navy has always been a navy of opportunism. Big risks had to be run, technically and tactically, and on balance they succeeded, though it is reported that on occasion, the vibration caused by the operation of diesel engines geared to shafts was embarrassing, particularly at the after end of the ship . . . [T]his super-technical battleship, fitted with no fewer than eight sets of engines, each of 6,750hp, each group of four driving a single shaft through gearing and an hydraulic coupling, which reduced the speed of the engine from 450 revolutions to 250 revolutions.

In addition to the overworked parts of the *Admiral Graf Spee*'s main engines, Langsdorff had additional worries, since his auxiliaries were failing too, along with the freezer plant. His armament on the other hand – and herein lay the provocative seed of Langsdorff's present dilemma – had barely been employed. This, combined with the fact that he had plenty of fuel with what he was just then taking (and with what would remain available in the *Altmark*) meant that, power plants permitting, he could cruise against the enemy for a further three months.

First then, his pen reiterated his basic orders; following this he went on to advance his new argument. The 'powerful artillery' of his ship 'can at least damage any anticipated enemy, except for the *Renown*, to such an extent that it is rendered ineffective as a shadower, and on the other hand that the hits that are to be expected *cannot significantly impair the return journey*', (my emphasis). In considering the British battlecruiser *Renown* his toughest opponent it is clear that, notwithstanding his own experience of air reconnaissance, he failed to fear the *Ark Royal*'s aircraft. In the event he did not have to: the lesson was to wait for the *Bismarck*'s sortie – but not before she had herself justified Langsdorff's basic premise by blowing to pieces the battlecruiser *Hood*.

In his appreciation, Langsdorff took comfort in the fact that his ship had sunk 28,125 gross registered tons of British shipping, a notable contribution 'to undermining before the world the English claim to unlimited command of the sea'. He had tied down immense enemy resources and forced much of the enemy's trade into convoy with all its 'inherent disadvantages'. That these would, in the end, prove less than its advantages, was at the time immaterial. For now Langsdorff declared his intention to strike again at the Cape route and then, if time and his engines permitted, dart west and hit the choke-point of the estuary of the Rio de la Plata. Among his officers were a number of reservists, men who had served in the German mercantile marine. One, Günther Schiebusch, afterwards recalled a conversation with Langsdorff during the middle-watch one night at the end of November and following the address Langsdorff had made to his officers on the 24th, Schiebusch 'ventured to ask [. . .] "Sir, don't you intend to go to the Plate? There some big meat or grain ships would certainly come our way."' At the time Langsdorff demurred, arguing the British had had time to send submarines 'to catch us there'. But the notion must have taken hold and Langsdorff's confidence and optimism had both impressed and concerned Rasenack. Perhaps it also convinced Langsdorff himself. At all events, he finally took refuge in the clause in his orders allowing the man-on-the-spot to select the best option 'if this furthers the main purpose of the operation'.

At the end of the day Langsdorff was the best judge and certainly he was not short of fire-eaters. His frustrated gunnery department were in support of his change of tune, eager for 'a fine finale to our cruise'.

In all this Langsdorff's isolation has to be taken into account. By his very admission to Dove he felt both remote from his officers and in need of human contact, even with an enemy national, no matter how empathetic the two men found themselves. True, he had distant counsel from Berlin, but behind the like-minded Raeder, there was the fearsome presence of Hitler. Arguments about Langsdorff's commitment to the Nazi cause have gone on since his death. What he felt in his heart died with him, but he served the Nazi state in its professional armed forces and his ship bore all the symbols of Nazism. Professor Eric Grove points out that:

Langsdorff seems to have welcomed Hitler's coming to power. The British captains who spoke to him in the *Graf Spee* found him to be a man of high ideals and, like virtually all German naval officers of his generation a convinced Nazi, 'though not rabidly so'. He took the 'Socialism' in 'National Socialism' seriously, and the British prisoners were intrigued at the 'very socialistic way' in which *Graf Spee* was run. The officers and men ate the same food and discipline was assessed as lax by British standards.

He can, however, have had little in common with the man who might have been his closest confidant, Heinrich Dau, of the *Altmark*. A convinced Nazi and Anglophobe, this 'dapper little man [. . .] his weather-beaten face tracing a lifetime at sea [. . .] an old-fashioned [imperial] beard now turning to grey [. . .] with cunning, lively eyes [. . .] was not popular with his officers'; nor with anyone else, for that matter, though his task running the passive but vital *Altmark* marked him too as a lonely figure.

Nor, despite his easy-going regime, did Langsdorff seem to have cultivated that symbiotic relationship with his operational staff officer and second-in-command, *Kapitän zur See* Kay, that might have eased his personal dilemma, but perhaps that was something inimical to the Nazi *Kriegsmarine*. Kay is described by Willi Frischauer and Robert Jackson as 'a queer mixture of devil-may-care-sea-dog almost in the British tradition, yet a strict disciplinarian who seemed to have little love for his cosmopolitan captain . . .' At the bottom of Langsdorff's motivation for taking a course of action that was to prove fatal for both himself and his ship, lay the matter of personal, professional ambition. His orders as a commerce raider were specific: to destroy and disrupt the enemy's trade and to do this he must, of necessity stay elusive, strike and disappear. Despite his ship's name, he was not another Graf von Spee, nor would there be, as he confided to Dove, either another Coronel or a Falklands. But then the business of running home, he knew, would undoubtedly run the high risk of an encounter with the enemy. If, as seemed to Langsdorff, in those hours of waiting for his ailing ship to complete her replenishment, this was not merely likely but inevitable, he must – in modern parlance – psych-up both himself and his ship's company. Himself so that he could conduct himself according to his personal idea of professional honour as a German naval officer; his crew so that they would bend to his will and rise to the challenge of testing themselves against an enemy with a fearsome reputation.

In the light of these reflections what Grove calls the 'Price of Disobedience' might seem, before the event, a currency worth the venturing. After all, Langsdorff commanded a puissant ship and, it is fair to say, he thought he could blast his way home.

Finally that day, the 28th, the gunnery officer *Fregattenkapitän* Ascher, and Ascher's deputy Rasenack took a turn around the ship in the cutter. Even while the replenishment had been under way, the ship's disguise had been completed and the officers went to inspect the result. For close quarters confusion, the ship's nameplates had been made to read *Deutschland*. The finishing touches had been made, breaking up the waterline with a high-speed bow wave and mid-length intermediate-wave being faked in white paint. 'The outline has changed radically . . .' Rasenack recorded. 'We are very pleased with our work.' It was a brilliant piece of deception.

Next morning the last act of the rendezvous was carried out and it was significant enough to indicate a major change of tack by Langsdorff even to the wretched British prisoners aboard *Altmark*. All the senior officers – masters, first mates, chief engineers and radio officers – and those wounded or injured, including 'two cases of severe toothache', in all twenty-seven men, were transferred from the *Altmark* to the *Admiral Graf Spee*. Finally, having arranged for Dau to support the *Admiral Graf Spee*'s last two thrusts at the enemy's shipping, Langsdorff ordered the *Altmark* to lay off. As the two ships drew apart Ascher and Rasenack calibrated their range-finding equipment and fine-tuned their gunnery-control system, then the two ships parted company. Thus, having made all possible preparations for every contingency, *Kapitän zur See* Langsdorff resumed his homeward cruise against the merchant shipping of the British Empire. On the last day of November and the first of December he headed east-north-east, towards the Cape route, aiming to strike it north-west of Walvis Bay, off the Namib coast in the vicinity of St Helena.

**The Allied Hunt**
**25 October–12 December: 'The Weakness of Our Intelligence . . .'**
Despite the frustration inherent in their hunt, the British had not been idle. Nor, for that matter, had their Allies. In the last seven days of October, a French *Force de Raide* under Admiral Gensoul, flying his flag in *Dunkerque*, with the cruisers *Georges Leygues, Montcalm* and *Gloire*; and the heavy destroyers *Mogador, Volta, L'Indomptable, Le Triomphant, Le Malin, La Fantasque, Le Terrible* and *L'Audacieux* in company, had been sweeping the Antilles–English Channel convoy route to cover Convoy KJ4 against attack by the *Deutschland*. On the 25th *La Fantasque* and *Le Terrible*, with the support of the cruiser *Dupleix*, had captured the German blockade running merchantman *Santa Fé*; a 4,627grt cargo liner belonging to the Hamburg-Südamerikanische Dampfschiffahrts Gesellschaft, she was taken into Dakar (to be returned to the German flag in 1940).

# The Allied Hunt: 25 October–12 December

Shortly afterwards Wells's Force K, as related earlier, operating from Freetown, had enjoyed the minor success of capturing the *Uhenfels* (taken into British service as the *Empire Ability* and sunk in Convoy SL76 by *U-69* in June 1941) on 5 November, but not much else until, that is, the report of the loss of the *Africa Shell* on the 15th. This had been preceded by a report by a South African trawler of a German warship 72 miles south of Cape Agulhas on the 10th. Although post-war analysis has tended to discount this from being a sighting of the *Admiral Graf Spee*, the fact that it was made at all indicates the threat as perceived by ordinary mariners. Whatever value was put on the report the situation was placed beyond all doubt after the *Africa Shell's* boats landed near Inhambane.

With the alarm raised on the extremity of his station, the British Commander-in-Chief of the East Indies, Vice Admiral R. Leatham, had formed hunting groups in the Indian Ocean. The battleships *Malaya* and *Ramillies*, with the aircraft carrier *Glorious* cruised off the Horn of Africa near Socotra. The carrier *Eagle* with the cruiser *Dorsetshire* and Australian destroyers *Vendetta* and *Waterhen* had been stationed south of Dondra Head, Ceylon (Sri Lanka); the British cruiser *Kent* and her French counterpart *Suffren*, with Australian destroyers *Vampire* and *Voyager* lay off the northern tip of Sumatra; while the Australian cruiser *Hobart* cruised along the trade route from Aden to Minicoy, off the southern tip of the India route. The British cruiser *Gloucester* and the French sloop *Rigault de Genouilly* covered an area from north of Madagascar towards the Seychelles, while the Australian destroyer *Stuart* and a submarine lay between the Maldives and the Chagos archipelago.

Elsewhere, on 14 November the French auxiliary cruiser *Koutoubia* had captured another Hansa Line ship, the 6,198 gross tons cargo ship *Trifels* near the Azores, but it was the important choke-point of trade off Cape Town, recognized from James Cook's day as the Tavern of the Oceans, that was suddenly vulnerable. With sinkings of merchant ships both to the west and now the east, reinforcing Force H, HM Cruisers *Shropshire* and *Sussex* was imperative. Accordingly the British Commander-in-Chief, South Atlantic, Vice Admiral D'Oyly Lyon, had despatched Force K from

Freetown, thus ironically sending the battlecruiser *Renown*, along with the aircraft carrier *Ark Royal* and the cruiser *Neptune*, towards the Cape; ironically because this would tend to increase the value of Langsdorff's disguise when he headed north. Wells's orders were to turn at the Cape and sweep north-west to Latitude 28° South, Longitude 15° West before returning to Freetown.

Success of a kind, however, went in the first instance to the British ships heading south. Receiving a report from the master of the Shaw Savill liner *Waimarama* on the 20th, the next day the *Neptune* intercepted the homeward-bound German passenger-cargo liner *Adolph Woermann* near Ascension Island. However, the *Neptune* was cheated of her prize as the Woermann liner was scuttled by her crew. Again, on 2 December, an aircraft of the South African Air Force – more irony, for she was a modified German Junkers Ju88 formerly owned by South African Airways – reported sighting a second Woermann liner, the *Watussi*. Reconnaissance flights by the SAAF had been made since the sinking of the *Trevannion* off Walvis Bay, the Ju88s of No. 16 B/R Squadron, SAAF, co-operating with HMSs *Sussex* and *Shropshire*. After the loss of the *Africa Shell* and

## HMS *EXETER*

A slightly older vessel than her consorts in the Battle of the River Plate, HMS *Exeter* was one of two modified County-class heavy cruisers known as the City-class. In *Exeter* and *York* X turret was dispensed with to produce a slightly cheaper and smaller vessel of 8,250 tons light displacement, rising to 10,410 fully laden. HMS *Exeter* was laid down at Devonport Dockyard, Plymouth, on 1 August 1928, launched on 18 July 1929 and commissioned on 27 July 1931.

She was 175 metres long, with a beam of 17.6 metres and a draught of 6.2 metres. Propulsion was produced from eight Admiralty three-drum boilers supplying four Parsons geared turbines driving four screws. The 80,000shp produced could drive her at a top speed of 32 knots. Her complement was 630 officers and ratings.

the transmission of the raider-warning from Durban, Durban-based No. 13 Squadron, SAAF, began flying up the coast towards Lourenço Marques – where German merchantmen were known to have sought refuge – and out to sea. With the warship of Forces K and H now united, No. 15 Squadron flew supporting air patrols to the southwards of Point Cape between 28 November and 2 December. It was by these means that the *Watussi* was located, the *Sussex* and *Renown* being sent to intercept her. She too was scuttled by her crew.

Meanwhile, off East Africa, with the carrier *Ark Royal* sent south towards the Cape of Good Hope, a second British aircraft carrier, HMS *Hermes*, was co-operating out of Dakar with the French cruisers *Dupleix* and *Foch*, while HM Submarine *Clyde* and the destroyers *Hardy*, *Hostile*, *Hasty* and *Hereward* patrolled the Freetown–Cape–Natal route, whither Langsdorff was now heading. Insofar as the informative *Waimarama*'s sister-ship *Tairoa* was concerned, the patrolling destroyers proved to be useless – as we shall shortly see.

The last of the Allied dispositions was Commodore Harwood's

As a 'heavy' cruiser, *Exeter* bore a main armament of six 8-inch (203mm) guns in three turrets (A and B forward, Y aft). The secondary armament as fitted consisted of four 4-inch high-angle anti-aircraft mountings with two 2-pounders. She also carried six 21-inch torpedo tubes in two amidships mountings. Her main armour comprised a belt of 3-inch, tapering to 2-inch steel; her decks were strengthened by 2-inch armour-plating with 2-inch to 1.5-inch on the gun houses, and 3-inch-thick armour on the conning tower.

For aerial reconnaissance she carried a catapult-launched Supermarine Walrus amphibian flying boat.

Like all cruisers of her generation, her armament was augmented as the war progressed. The *Exeter* was lost in the Battle of the Java Sea as part of an Allied task force commanded by the Dutch admiral, Karel Doorman.

# The Battle of the River Plate

Force G, whose operational area was north of the Falkland Islands, off the long coastline of South America. This consisted of four cruisers, the *Ajax*, *Achilles*, *Exeter* and *Cumberland*, the latter pair of which were, at the beginning of December, both at Port Stanley 'in case the enemy should conceive the idea of attacking it on the anniversary of the Falkland Islands battle on the 8 December 1914; the *Achilles* was off Rio de Janeiro and the *Ajax* had recently sailed from Port Stanley for the River Plate' (the Rio de la Plata). While three of Harwood's cruisers were to prove Langsdorff's nemesis, this was far from clear on the 2 December as the Admiralty strove to draw the net round the quarry.

In knowing the outcome of the eventual collision of Langsdorff and Harwood, it is as easy to lose sight of the immense forces ranged in search of the German warship, as it is to appreciate that they covered a quarter of the globe in their extent. Despite this the British Admiralty staff was perplexed. 'The weakness of our intelligence regarding the movement of major enemy vessels to and from home waters,' recorded the official naval historian Captain Stephen Roskill, 'thus reflected itself in distant operations.' As for the Naval Intelligence Department, its official historian, Professor F.H. Hinsley, admitted that: 'The engagement which led to the destruction of the *Graf Spee* [. . .] was brought about without any assistance from the N[aval] I[ntelligence [D]epartment . . .'

Notwithstanding the British and French effort, which, it must be remembered, included aircraft from South Africa and warships from Australia and New Zealand (most of which carried Walrus amphibious reconnaissance aircraft as useful and more serviceable to the Allies than Langsdorff's Arado floatplane), Langsdorff was still able to hide his ship and his support vessel in the vast wastes of the South Atlantic.

## The *Admiral Graf Spee*
### 2–12 December: 'No Alternative but to Obey'
So far that tide in the affairs of men that leads on to fortune had run in Langsdorff's favour, and he was yet to enjoy some hours of flood. The forenoon of 2 December was clear with light winds, a sharp,

bright day with perfect visibility. At noon, when some 650 miles east of St Helena, Langsdorff catapulted the patched-up Arado, equally eager to locate a target as to keep watch for a British cruiser. With the floatplane airborne and heading south, smoke was sighted to the north-east through the powerful Zeiss masthead range-finding optics at something in excess of 50 kilometres. Recalling Bongard and his aeroplane – though without awaiting its return – Langsdorff headed at full speed towards the smudge of smoke. A little under an hour later the upperworks of a merchantman were reported, ruling out the possibility of a man-of-war. Although she might yet prove to be an Armed Merchant Cruiser, Langsdorff was taking no chances, the alarms rang and, with his crew at action stations, Langsdorff ordered Ascher and Rasenack to lay their guns on the target. Then came the order: 'Schuht!'

The British Blue Star cargo liner *Doric Star* was homeward-bound from Australia and New Zealand by way of the Cape of Good Hope. Loaded 'with a full refrigerated cargo of mutton, lamb, cheese and butter [. . .] with a quantity of wool in bales in her 'tween decks, slicing through the calm sea a long, low swell at 12 knots'. The noon position having been found a little earlier, Captain William Stubbs had just finished his lunch when, like Mr A.E. Willis, the second officer on watch and the duty lookout, Able Seaman Tom Foley, he heard the whine and then explosion of a shell, which struck the water 'within 100 yards of the *Doric Star*'. A shaken Foley watched the tall column of white water rise on the starboard bow. Rushing to the bridge Stubbs ordered action stations, then grabbed his binoculars and, with his watch officer, scanned the horizon. 'A couple of minutes later a vessel was sighted about a point on the port quarter. At about 1.10 p.m. a second shell exploded within 200 yards off the starboard bow, and the overtaking vessel was seen to be a battleship.' Debris from the shell casing hit the ship. What Stubbs could see was no more than the tall forebridge of the *Admiral Graf Spee* but it was enough. Having immediately 'ordered the Wireless Operator (Mr William Comber) to transmit the raider distress call' and called for the engine room to give him 'all possible speed' Stubbs realized that:

# The Battle of the River Plate

**SS *Doric Star***

After the second shot [. . .] it was impossible to escape, so [I] stopped the engines and ordered the wireless operator to amplify the message and state battleship attacking. By this time I could read the daylight Morse lamp from [the] battleship signalling 'Stop your wireless!' but I took no notice [. . .] As the battleship approached I gave orders to the engine room to stand by for scuttling, and as it appeared that our distress call had not been heard I ordered [the] Chief Engineer (Mr W. Ray) to start and scuttle. A few minutes later the wireless operator reported that our message had been repeated by another British vessel and also a Greek vessel, so I countermanded the orders for scuttling then threw overboard all confidential papers and books, breech of gun, ammunition and rifles, also all papers about cargo. After [the] distress call had been transmitted I ordered the wireless operator to cease transmitting as the [fast approaching] battleship was exhibiting a notice 'Stop you[r] wireless or I will open fire.'

The *Doric Star*, a 12-knot ship with one anti-submarine gun right aft, had no alternative but to obey.

Bringing the *Admiral Graf Spee* to, with her guns commanding the cargo liner, Langsdorff despatched his boarding party. Three officers, led by *Oberleutnant* Bruno Herzberg, and accompanied by 'about 30 men', boarded the *Doric Star*. Herzberg was a naval reserve officer with extensive experience of merchant ships, having been a peacetime chief officer in the Hamburg-Amerika Linie. This and the fact that he spoke excellent English, commended him to Langsdorff as boarding and prize-officer. Herzberg's well-trained and by now well-practised party scrambled all over the *Doric Star*:

> They dispersed to various parts of the ship with drawn revolvers – the bridge, the wireless room and engine room. The captain was taken to his cabin and closely examined. The wireless room was searched for codes and cyphers, and the radio officer asked if he had sent out his position, to which he replied that of course he had . . .

Stubbs concealed the fact that his ship carried anything other than wool. This appeared to be confirmed when the tarpaulins were removed and the hatch-boards lifted, for the 'tween decks were stuffed with the oily and smelly bales. In the interim Chief Engineer Ray had sufficiently disabled the engines to dissuade the Germans from seizing the *Doric Star* as a prize. Langsdorff was understandably in a hurry to quit the scene of his latest raid and had, moreover, just received a report from Bongard that the Arado had run out of fuel and was sitting on the broad bosom of the South Atlantic with a damaged float. Accordingly, Herzberg had told his victims they had ten minutes to gather personal possessions before they would be taken off their ship.

Meanwhile the boarding party looted 'sextants, chronometers, binoculars, telescopes and even typewriters', as they hustled the *Doric Star*'s crew into the boats. They also found some silver ingots in Stubbs's cabin, valuable cargo being carried 'per favour of the master'. A few demolition charges were set, but failed to sink the Blue Star liner. Once Langsdorff had recovered his boats he ordered her sunk by his secondary armament. This failed to despatch the *Doric Star* quickly and, in the end, it took two torpedoes to administer the *coup de grâce*.

# The Battle of the River Plate

Radio intercepts confirmed that the *Doric Star*'s distress signal had been picked up by six ships, one of them the British cargo liner *Port Chalmers* and this must have kindled renewed anxiety in Langsdorff, an anxiety that must have been compounded by the delay in locating the ditched Arado. Nor did it now help to learn that, far from being full of wool and notwithstanding the cache of silver, the *Doric Star* had contained the meat and dairy products the *Panzerschiff* stood most in need of: the gilt was rubbing off the triumph. Did Langsdorff, with that preternatural sense that often imbues those in isolated command, feel the chill sense of foreboding? Perhaps, but it must have preyed on his mind that he was tarrying too long in the area, for it took the remainder of the day for a bad-tempered Langsdorff to find and recover the floatplane and its *Luftwaffe* pilot; then, as darkness fell, he headed south-west.

Langsdorff's choice of track was an approximate right-angle to the Cape Town–Freetown rhumb-line, gaining him the greatest distance from it and any British cruiser squadron that might be patrolling it – as indeed Admiral Wells was. But it also yielded another victim, one which had been sighted the previous day by Bongard before he was compelled to ditch the Arado. This was a serendipitous conjunction for Langsdorff, perhaps an indication that the fates still smiled upon his enterprise, though he appears to have been in an unusually fractious mood, annoyed about the Arado, annoyed that Stubbs had fooled his boarding officer about the nature of the *Doric Star*'s cargo, annoyed that the Blue Star liner had so competently revealed the attack as it was happening, and annoyed that it had immediately been picked up by other ships.

By dawn the *Admiral Graf Spee* was south-east of St Helena and 170 miles away from the position of the *Doric Star*'s shattered hull. Aboard the *Panzerschiff*, daylight seemed to confirm the anticipation raised by Bongard's report of the previous evening for, as the optical rangefinder operators took a sweep round the horizon in the growing light, smoke was sighted 13 miles away on the port quarter 'against the clear morning sky'. Running aloft the French tricolour Langsdorff turned his ship, increased speed, and ordered a course to intercept the new quarry.

# The *Admiral Graf Spee*: 2-12 December

SS *Tairoa*

Mr F.J. Cummins, radio officer of the British cargo liner *Tairoa* had been one of those who heard the *Doric Star*'s distress signal on 2 December; the information was quickly passed to the ship's bridge. On being informed of the presence of a strike in the vicinity of his intended homeward track, Captain W.B.S. Starr ordered an alteration of course to the westwards, hoping thereby to avoid the enemy. It was an unfortunate decision for the *Tairoa*, but Starr 'didn't know the nature of the raider. She might have been an armed merchant cruiser, a submarine or a pocket battleship'. Starr left orders to be called at 04.00 on the 3rd and 'half an hour later, with the first streak of dawn in the sky, a faint smudge [of smoke] appeared. It was the *Graf Spee* . . .'

The *Tairoa* grossed 7,983 tons and was owned by the Shaw, Savill and Albion Co Ltd's subsidiary, the Norfolk and North American Steam Shipping Co Ltd, all part of the giant Furness Withy Group. She was, besides personal effects and other small consignments of general cargo, full of mutton, wool and lead loaded in Australia. On her way home, the *Tairoa* had called at Durban for fuel and mail, leaving on 27 November for Freetown where, like the *Doric Star*, she was scheduled to join a homeward convoy. Frederick Cummins was a middle-aged veteran of the First World War, during which he had been torpedoed and mined several times; the news he had passed to his commander, William Starr, had kept the *Tairoa*'s master in a state of anxiety throughout the night, for Starr knew that another Shaw, Savill and Albion ship, the *Ceramic*, was not far away and the Union-Castle mail liner, the *Sterling Castle*, with women and children among her passengers, was not far astern of the *Tairoa*.

# The Battle of the River Plate

Langsdorff's mood had not improved. According to Frischauer and Jackson, he was worried lest the *Tairoa* got off a warning radio signal. As the *Admiral Graf Spee* ran her victim down and her alarms were calling her crew to action stations he told his officers he wanted 'quick action' and would tolerate no nonsense from the enemy. They were to open fire immediately upon the interception of any wireless transmission.

'The battleship closed in on us very quickly,' reported Starr. When 2 miles distant from her quarry the French ensign was replaced by the German *Swastika* and the signal to stop was accompanied by a shot across the *Tairoa*'s bows. Starr immediately ordered the ship's position passed to Cummins with an order to transmit a raider warning and that the *Tairoa* was being: 'Attacked by German battleship *Admiral Scheer*. A bad guess on my part!'

Aboard the *Admiral Graf Spee* the reaction was swift. Cummins had just completed the first transmission when the first shell from the *Panzerschiff*'s secondary armament hit the *Tairoa*'s upperworks. Betrayed by the upward leading wires of his aerials, Cummins himself was the target in his sandbagged wireless room, though the shell had passed through a cabin accommodating a supernumerary officer. Coolly, Cummins repeated the message scribbled before him with its precise intersection of parallel and meridian: Latitude 21° 38' South, Longitude 003° 13' West, as more shells slammed into the ship, starting fires. One tore through the radio room bulkhead 'wrecking the [radio] set Cummins was using, but Cummins scrambled away unhurt', making for the bridge and joining Starr, the chief steward and Third Officer F.J. Paterson, the last named taking the wheel from a rattled quartermaster.

This turned out to be useless. 'Immediately the wireless started the *Graf Spee* opened fire on us, shells bursting on the bridge, Captain's cabin, officers' quarters and wireless room. One wing of the bridge was wrecked, the steering gear put out of action and the port boats badly damaged . . .'

Starr had already ditched his confidential documents and he was now informed that five of his people were wounded by splinters. Three were deck-boys, one of whom had been injured seriously in the thigh. Bowing to the overwhelming force ranged against him, he stopped his ship, ordering the boats lowered as the *Admiral Graf Spee* closed the *Tairoa*'s port side and strafed her with machine-gun fire, holing all but the two starboard lifeboats. These, however, were clumsily lowered under the direction of the chief officer, Mr F.M. Murphy, and pulled clear of the ship before all hands had been embarked. Covered by this murderous fire Langsdorff sent away his motor boats and boarding party under Herzberg. One of these made for the boats, ordering them to return alongside the *Tairoa*, the other ran alongside the dangling boat-falls, the armed Germans scrambling up the obligingly lowered lifeboat boarding ladders.

Again, quick thinking on the part of the *Tairoa*'s now wounded chief steward, J.C. Smith deceived the Germans as to the nature of the ship's cargo. 'Coal,' Smith told them when asked. Although the hatches were not lifted, the boarding party looted the storerooms and discovered eighteen bottles of carbonic acid, which proved a boon for the *Admiral Graf Spee*'s failing refrigeration machinery. Meanwhile the *Tairoa*'s shaken evacuees, many of them her lascar complement, reboarded their ship while the lifeboats were ordered cast adrift. After a muster the *Tairoa*'s people were given ten minutes to gather their belongings before being conveyed to the *Admiral Graf Spee* by the German warship's motor boats.

Here Starr and Cummins (Frederick Cummins was afterwards awarded the MBE for his gallantry in continuing to transmit) were interviewed by Langsdorff, who 'typically' congratulated them on their gallantry, though it had frustrated his intentions. The British masters – civilians under international law and certainly in Langsdorff's opinion – simply would not conform to the game as he wished it to be humanely played. Meanwhile, the *Tairoa*'s mixed crew were encountering the other prisoners. In all there were now 196 incarcerated aboard the *Panzerschiff*. Of the officers Captain A. Brown, master of the *Huntsman* recalled: 'We were now fifty-one in one small room. Packed, without room to sit, we ate our meals in relays.' Five of the *Tairoa*'s men were wounded, including two boys. The *Admiral Graf Spee*'s fire had been efficient and purposeful; those aboard the *Admiral Graf Spee* heard 'what sounded like 5.9-inch guns. Next came the "pom-pom-pom" of a heavy machine gun . . .' , other accounts mention 'sixty shells'. Whatever his private desires and Starr's subsequent assertion that Langsdorff had 'used only his smallest [calibre] guns to achieve his purpose [which] helped to keep casualties to a minimum', Langsdorff's reputation for not having killed a single British merchant seaman was purely circumstantial.

Before leaving the scene Langsdorff sank the *Tairoa* with six shells from his secondary armament and a torpedo. Then, increasing speed, the *Admiral Graf Spee* headed west, for it was Langsdorff's intention now to cross the South Atlantic and strike at trade on the coast of South America, near Rio de Janeiro. On the way he would rendezvous once more with *Altmark*, divest himself of the bulk of the prisoners, and top up with fuel and ammunition.

During the run west, on 4 December, Langsdorff received intelligence from Berlin: it was a mixed bag both encouraging and worrying. Diplomatic sources in Montevideo had informed the *Oberkommando der Kriegsmarine* that Harwood's Force G was active in the vicinity of the Rio de la Plata, but the squadron was divided. One of Harwood's cruisers, HMNZS *Achilles*, was still lying alongside in Montevideo with every appearance of remaining there for a while. More important, however, was the news that the Royal Mail Line's *Highland Monarch* and the Blue Star Line's *Andalucia Star* had almost completed their loading and would be leaving between the 5th and the 8th. As a light cruiser of the *Leander*-class, Langsdorff had little to fear from the *Achilles*'s 6-inch main armament, should she attempt to cover the departure of the two valuable and loaded British liners. If the remainder of Harwood's ships were dispersed, as the situation-report indicated, he could make a lightning strike, which would be both materially and morally damaging to the enemy's cause. Indeed, this was precisely the encounter for which he had redefined the purpose of his cruise. Now he had no time to lose.

The news made vital swift replenishment from the *Altmark*. The two ships met on Wednesday, 6 December in Latitude 27° 30' South, Longitude 019° 45' West. Conditions were ideal in the high Austral summer: bright sunshine and a moderate sea generated by the south-

SS *Andalucia Star*

easterly Trade Wind. The *Admiral Graf Spee* picked up the *Altmark*'s trailing line and oil-hose without difficulty. The great grey ship followed astern in the wake of the tanker, both moving slowly westwards, the motor boats effecting the transfer of stores, ammunition and prisoners as they did so. Langsdorff retained on board his ship the masters, chief officers, chief engineers, radio officers, plus the chief refrigerating engineers of the *Doric Star* and the *Tairoa*, skilled men who might prove useful to the Fatherland if he got them back to Germany – or so it was believed aboard the *Panzerschiff*. Also retained aboard were an assistant engineer from the *Huntsman* and the three worst of the wounded deck-boys from the *Tairoa*, a total of twenty-nine. There were two exceptions among the masters: Captain Brown of the *Huntsman* and Captain Starr of the *Tairoa*, both of whom were ordered to accompany and tend their apprehensive lascars aboard the *Altmark*. The two masters spoke Urdu and were trusted by their Indian sailors, men for whom their Nazi captors had little sympathy and less inclination to understand.

The new intake of 144 prisoners was not welcomed by Dau, who appears to have doubted Langsdorff's motives and, more significantly, his political commitment. Nevertheless, in Langsdorff's cabin, over a customary glass of *Schnapps*, the two men discussed the replenishment of the *Altmark*'s tanks by the German tanker *Tacoma*, then loading in Montevideo. They also made contingent plans for further meetings off Tristan da Cunha. As twilight approached and the work was concluded with the two ships separating, Ascher asked if he might test the focus of his searchlights, and at dawn the following morning requested that *Altmark* tow a target for a gunnery exercise. This was approved by Langsdorff and Dau returned to the *Altmark*, where he received reports of disorderly behaviour among the prisoners, as those on board welcomed the diversion of new arrivals. Concerned about now having some 300 enemy seamen on board – about twice the number of his own crew – Dau decided to muster the prisoners next day.

After dark the *Admiral Graf Spee*'s searchlight operators carried out their exercise. 'This is very necessary,' wrote Rasenack, 'since the adroit manipulation of the searchlights is of the first importance for one's own security and the effectiveness of our guns.' Shortly after completion of this, with the hands stood down, the alarms rang. A darkened merchant ship was seen passing to starboard on a reciprocal course. 'Has the light of our searchlights attracted some moth?' Rasenack wondered, expecting Langsdorff to annihilate the ship along with all possibility of discovery. He did nothing, to the 'general disappointment' of many.

Although the stranger was almost certainly British (neutrals usually showing as many lights as possible), Langsdorff expressed the possibility that it might be a German vessel – possibly the *Windhoek* – 'navigating away from the usual routes attempting to return to Germany'. If not, and the ship was British, the Captain, fearing a warning signal would hazard his planned operation, guessed that his luck had held and that the *Admiral Graf Spee* had no more been seen at a distance as she had been in passing close. Unlike a man-of-war, which had numerous men closed up, even at cruising stations, a merchantman making a passage well offshore would have at most but three men on watch, one of whom would be the helmsman concentrating on the compass before him. An attack might spark a warning signal and then a hue-and-cry, causing Harwood to concentrate his dispersed forces against the German raider. Moreover, any engagement might not only compromise the opportunity for greater prizes off the Rio de la Plata, but the identity of his supply ship. Finally, night actions introduced an element of uncertainty inimical to Langsdorff's *modus operandi*.

Rasenack was not so sure. To him Langsdorff's action was counter-intuitive. He recorded in his diary 'a foreboding. In my view, the best way to ensure that we remain unrecognized was to sink that ship as quickly as possible, to blaze at her deck with guns of all calibre so that she should not be able to send out a distress signal.'

Aboard *Altmark* early next morning, Dau read the riot act to the assembled British, under the guns of the *Admiral Graf Spee*. The German captain's address was, to the listening British, an underwhelming performance and it seems to have been terminated by a signal from the *Admiral Graf Spee* cancelling the gunnery exercise. With a stream of bright bunting signalling 'Auf Wiedersehen', the *Panzerschiff* made off to the westwards at high speed, leaving her patient *milch-cow* in her wake: until the next time . . .

Some hours after the valedictory signal to the *Altmark* had been hauled down aboard the *Admiral Graf Spee*, the French tricolour was once more run up. It was by now 17.46 – late afternoon – and another potential victim was in sight, one that could be silenced before dark. She was the *Streonshalh* – her name was the Viking one for her home port of Whitby – a tramp steamer of 3,895 gross tons owned by Headlam and Sons' subsidiary Rowland and Marwood's Steamship Co Ltd. She had brought a cargo of Tyne coal outwards and was loaded with 5,654 tons of Uruguayan wheat for the homeward run, by way of Freetown, where she would join a convoy.

Langsdorff's destruction of the *Streonshalh* was swift. He fell upon the unsuspecting tramp, whose master, Captain J.J. Robinson, 'was sitting on the lower bridge reading' when the chief officer 'said he thought he had seen a sailing ship on the horizon. I went up to the top bridge and put my telescope on her and made her out to be the fighting top of a cruiser'. At first Robinson thought the newcomer a British warship but, although he kept the *Streonshalh* on course, he 'took no chances' getting all hands on deck to swing the boats out and place extra provisions in them.

# The Battle of the River Plate

**SS** *Streonshalh*

Again Langsdorff approached end-on and flying the French ensign. 'She steamed right round on to my course and then at last I observed she was German.' The *Admiral Graf Spee* was within half a mile of the tramp when the *Swastika* was run up. Now Robinson could read the signals the warship was flying: 'If you transmit on your wireless I will open fire immediately.' He ordered his watch-officer to grab the confidential books and get rid of them, then he rang the engine room telegraph astern to take the way off the ship and ordered the crew to the boats. The *Streonshalh*'s people cast loose the boats, which were soon in the water. So too were those of the German raider, whose occupants were swiftly swarming up the side of the British tramp as she slowed to a stop, eager to ransack the bridge and cabins and 'conduct the usual fruitless search for secret papers or anything else [. . .] [that] might be of use'. Robinson had undergone the same experience in the previous war. On the *Streonshalh*'s bridge he grabbed the routeing instructions, tore them up and stirred them into a can of paint left on the bridge when routine work had ceased for the day. He failed, however, to prevent the German boarding party discovering a copy of the *Buenos Aires Herald* in the chief engineer's cabin.

The *Streonshalh*'s boats were rounded up, the officers remaining on board the tramp steamer were taken off and all were brought aboard

unching of the *Admiral Graf Spee* at Wilhelmshaven, 30 June 1934.

ptain Hans Langsdorff (Dr Reinhard Langsdorff).  Commodore Harwood, pictured in 1936.

Watercolour sketch of the *Admiral Graf Spee*, made from the *Huntsman* by Lieutenant Ulpts.

The *Admiral Graf Spee*'s 11-inch guns at maximum elevation.

The *Admiral Graf Spee* camouflaged as a British battlecruiser with a dummy B turret.

The *Admiral Graf Spee*'s control tower.

The *Admiral Graf Spee* in Hamburg before the war.

*Ajax* firing a salvo, as seen from the *Achilles*.

An early photograph of HMS *Achilles* in 1933.

An aerial shot of the *Graf Spee* at Montevideo.

The *Admiral Graf Spee* and the *Tacoma* in Montevideo harbour after the battle.

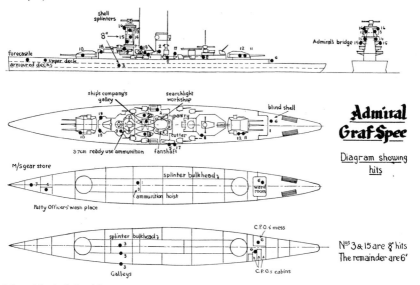

The *Admiral Graf Spee* at Montevideo between 14 and 17 December 1939.

Diagram of the *Admiral Graf Spee* .

Twenty to thirty seconds after the first big explosion, which scuttled the *Admiral Graf Spee*.

The wreck of the *Admiral Graf Spee* burning.

Wreck of the *Admiral Graf Spee* still smoking at sunrise next day.

Final paragraph of the *Admiral Graf Spee*'s log, signed by the Executive Officer, Captain Kay in Buenos Aires. The text reads: 'The moral effect of Captain Langsdorff's suicide on Argentine public opinion is extraordinary and extends also to circles unfriendly to us up till now.'

```
Die moralische Auswirkung des Freitodes von Kapitän
zur See Langsdorff auf die argentinische Oeffentlichkeit ist
ausserordentlich und erstreckt sich zum Teil auch auf uns
bisher feindlich gesinnte Kreise.
                                        gez Kay.
```

Captain Langsdorff gives the naval salute at the funeral of the thirty-seven German seamen killed in action.

Funeral of Captain Langsdorff.

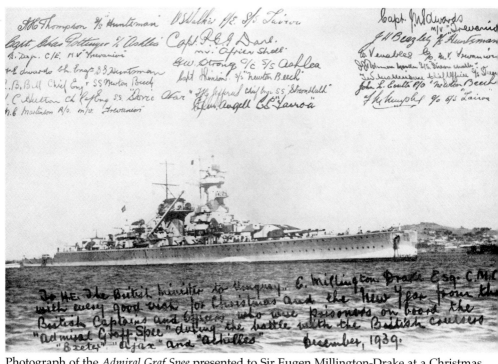

Photograph of the *Admiral Graf Spee* presented to Sir Eugen Millington-Drake at a Christmas dinner by some of the merchant captains who were prisoners in the *Graf Spee* during the battle

HMS *Exeter*.

the *Admiral Graf Spee*. The *Streonshalh*'s crew were accommodated 'in a room forward'. Robinson and his chief officer were

> taken to the navigator's cabin, where two officers, one of whom was Lieutenant Herzberg, gave us a glass of beer, and tried to find out about the routes from the Plate to Freetown. We had, it [was] true, been routed from the Plate, but we were miles off the ordinary route. I told him that I did not know anything about routes at all as we were not following any special route.

Claims were later made about one of the ditched confidential bags having floated, and by its capture, revealing information which persuaded Langsdorff that a point 300 miles east of the estuary of the Rio de la Plata was a focal point in British Admiralty routeing for merchant ships. Although Robinson afterwards disputed the truth of the capture, post-event analysis suggested that one bag may have been recovered, though through no fault of Robinson's. The Germans seem to have made some deductions from one of the *Streonshalh*'s officer's sight-books, though again Robinson refuted this, stating that no records were kept. Robinson did not, however, deny the capture of the *Buenos Aires Herald*, which, as we shall note, *did* have its influence on events.

Captain Robinson and his officers made up a total of thirty-one masters and officers, plus the three wounded lads, in the after space set aside for them. Ten shells from the secondary armament sent the *Streonshalh* to the bottom in Latitude 25° 01' South, Longitude 027° 50' West.

In his cabin Langsdorff studied the *Buenos Aires Herald*. The captured English-language newspaper contained the latest shipping news, confirming the sailings from the Rio de la Plata. The *Highland Monarch* had indeed left on the 5th and the intelligence from Berlin was corroborated, for the *Andalucia Star* was also due to sail. But so too was a small convoy of four vessels and although this might possibly be escorted by British warships, any such escort would not amount to a man-of-war with superior gunpower to Langsdorff's own.

Armed with whatever material had been gleaned from the sunken *Streonshalh* and consulting the charts with his senior navigating officer, *Korvettenkapitän* Jürgen Wattenberg, Langsdorff calculated or guessed – or at least *believed* – that his best striking point was about 300 miles east-north-east of the wide estuary of the Rio de la Plata. (Whatever the truth, the German officers were convinced that they had discovered an important point in the secret British route towards the convoy assembly port of Freetown, Sierra Leone. According to Rasenack, it meant altering their future rendezvous positions with the *Altmark*.) Word was passed to the bridge and a course laid accordingly. Shortly after leaving the site of the *Streonshalh*'s sinking, the *Admiral Graf Spee* crossed the boundary of the Pan-American Neutrality Zone, abandoning any easy pickings south of Rio de Janeiro and heading for the greater concentration of targets anticipated off the Rio de la Plata.

SS *Highland Monarch*

Next morning the Arado, its damaged float mended, was catapulted into the air. The sorties became twice-daily highlights for the British officers mewed up below the catapult's position, morning and evening flights being made during the 8th, 9th and 10th as the *Admiral Graf Spee* motored south-west. Every launch meant the possibility of another British ship being sunk and, while they welcomed new faces – Robinson's arrival confirmed they had crossed the Atlantic and were now preying on the South American trade routes – the losses of shipping were depressing. But then, on the morning of 11 December the revving of the Arado's BMW engine failed; silence ensued: the floatplane was useless. The British merchant naval officers were cheered at the set-back; Langsdorff accepted the news stoically. There was nothing he could do about it, though to be deprived of his long-range 'eyes' at such a moment was a disappointment. Besides, he was musing on other considerations, the emerging convoy in particular, which Berlin informed Langsdorff would total 30,000 tons, over half his tonnage sunk to date and exceeding the total sunk by Graf Von Luckner in SMS *Emden* in the First World War. Of course, it might be escorted by an Armed Merchant Cruiser, even perhaps *Achilles* and a pair of destroyers; if such were to be the case, and his carefully argued appreciation was to be worked-out, it behove him to have his ship in a state of the highest readiness.

He ordered Kay to pass word to dismantle the dummy funnel and the phoney gun turret, for they might compromise his fire control in an action involving several targets, as would be the case if he fell upon a convoy. Rasenack gives us a final insight into Langsdorff's fateful thinking as he mused on the fates of other German warships in these waters:

Our Captain [. . .] had arrived at the conclusion that a ship like ourself operating alone from her base must never approach too close to a coast nor enter waters which could be controlled from bases on land. All the German ships which had done so in the First World War had found such an approach had always been the beginning of the end. Up till now in all our movements our Captain was faithful to his principles, although the possibilities of finding [enemy merchant] ships in the middle of the ocean were few. For him above all the safety of the ship was his first consideration. Only now as he was seeking the opportunity of a successful finale before setting out on his return did he go all out and risk everything.

They continued their search 'along the route which the *Streonshalh* had taken from the Plate', expecting to encounter the *Highland Monarch* on the 10th, but 'found nothing', though the Royal Mail liner had sailed at 15.08 on 6 December and was about two days behind the *Streonshalh*. 'Nothing happens' on the 11th either.

On the evening of Sunday, 12 December Langsdorff wrote up his night orders. Although they had seen nothing since the *Streonshalh* to the south of Trinidad, they had closed to within 150 miles of the Brazilian coast and he now ordered a turn offshore to quarter his chosen cruising ground. Then he went below to his sea cabin and turned in, expecting to be roused as usual just before dawn next morning.

### 13 December, Midnight–06.17: 'A Fine Target'

Langsdorff slept through the middle watch on the 13th December as his ship cruised south-south-east at 15 knots. We do not know his state of mind, but he might rest as soundly as any commander on active service, for he had notched up a total of nine ships amounting to a gross registered tonnage of 50,089 tons and could dream of exceeding the *Emden*'s bag on the morrow. This cumulative measure of capacity lost to the British certainly indicates the amount of hard assets he and his crew had destroyed, but one must also consider the sheer bulk of commodities lost: the *Ashlea*'s sugar, the *Streonshalh*'s grain, the frozen meat and chilled dairy products of the *Doric Star* and the *Tairoa*, the *Newton Beech*'s maize, the *Huntsman*'s general cargo with its quantities of jute, tea, ore and gum, the *Trevannion*'s ore and even the petrol, kerosene and general cargo being exported in the *Clement*. All were debits to the British economy. While detractors of this method of commerce raiding argue the game was not worth the candle – for the ultimate expense to Germany was high – and compares unfavourably with the lower investment and higher achievement possible with a U-boat, Langsdorff had effected a degree of material success to which may be added the immeasurable compound effects of tying down British naval forces in the hunt for him, a factor in the planning of such commerce raiding cruises. Along with causing frustration in the Royal Navy, there was a corresponding erosion in any faith the British Merchant Service had in its nominal protector, along with which went a consequent drop in morale. Certainly, in contrast to his colleague Wennecker in the *Deutschland*, he remained top of his class and, at this early stage of the war, a veritable star of the *Kriegsmarine*.

Although, of course, we have no idea of his thinking, his very presence off the Rio de la Plata, argues an anticipation of more rich pickings among the British shipping passing through that focal point. Moreover, to his officers he was irrepressibly optimistic when called next morning and, apparently, convinced of his good fortune.

Taking their customary sweep of the lightening horizon as the dawning day slowly grew to full light, the range-finding operators high above the *Admiral Graf Spee*'s navigating bridge spotted a tall, thin mast breaking the perfect line marking the edge of the visible world at a distance of 31,000 metres, some 15.5 nautical miles, on the starboard bow. The actual sighting at 05.52 was attributed to *Leutnant zur See* Grigat. *Kapitän* Langsdorff was informed and the opinion on the bridge of the *Panzerschiff* was rapidly formed that they were not the sturdy, derrick-bearing spars of a merchantman, but the elevated, aerial-spreading masts of warships. In response Langsdorff passed word to maintain course and speed.

As he dressed, Langsdorff seems to have assumed with a confidence that indeed bespoke a good night's sleep and a fair judgement on his enemy's position and timing, that the masts probably belonged to the light cruiser *Achilles* and a brace of destroyers escorting the small but valuable convoy he had been expecting. A few minutes later he was on the bridge, *Korvettenkapitän* Wattenberg, his navigator beside him.

As other senior officers were summoned further reports came down: the mast was almost certainly that of a cruiser; then there were more masts, moving from right to left, at which point Langsdorff now concluded – absolutely in his own mind – that the first was indeed that of *Achilles* and the others belonged to two destroyers. Both Kay and Wattenberg were now with him and Langsdorff was advised, or politely reminded, of the *Seekriegsleitung*'s specific orders to avoid tangling with a superior enemy force. He could still break away, for the unknown ships seemed to be crossing ahead of the *Admiral Graf Spee* in ignorance of her presence. Kay apparently suggested they slowed down and allowed the strangers to pass. Langsdorff demurred, giving his opinion that the enemy warships had a convoy under their wing and that as defending men-of-war they were inferior to their own ship and their own firepower. That their captain regarded the sightings as a worthwhile target was in no doubt, though it appears to have run counter to his subordinate colleagues' intuition. However, it fell in with Langsdorff's assessment and his expressed desire to make his mark against the enemy's naval power. With a curt order, the captain of the *Admiral Graf Spee* ordered an interception and engagement.

The alarm bells rang at 06.00, turning out the watches-below and sending them to their action stations. On a false assumption, Langsdorff had committed himself, his ship and his ship's company. Self-confidence – perhaps even hubris – had led him to disregard his orders, even in the face of nemesis. If, as his advocates claim, his subsequent actions saved the lives of a thousand men, these two initial errors were to condemn a hundred to death.

In terms of enemy tonnage sunk the success of Langsdorff's cruise might be arguable; in its tying down of enemy forces it had been supremely successful. As we have seen no less than eight Anglo-French so-called 'hunting-groups' had been formed, further draining Allied, but largely British, resources, wearing out ships and men and consuming fuel. The widely spread net had caught some German merchantmen running the blockade, but these were essentially minnows: the shark had remained tantalizingly, frustratingly, at large.

The Allied response to the presence of one or two dangerous raiders at large on the high seas had originated from a meeting on 4 October chaired by the British First Sea Lord, Sir Dudley Pound. As we have observed, the British assessment of the dispositions of German commerce raiders was flawed, confused by the *Deutschland*'s sinking of the *Stonegate*, the *Clement*'s master's report that his ship had been sunk by the *Admiral Scheer* and this ship also being attributed with the sinking of the *Rawalpindi*. Although shipping was already in convoy in the North Atlantic and such convoys had been beefed-up with big-gun escorts, this was patchy and largely obsolete, consisting of the old R-class battleships *Resolution* and *Revenge*, a brace of light cruisers

(*Emerald* and *Enterprise*) and some Armed Merchant Cruisers, which tragically proved no match for major German warships. Insufficient assets were available to place all Allied merchant shipping in convoy and outside the North Atlantic merchant ships would have to take their chance. They were expendable and losses inevitable, though of course great things were expected from the aggressive hunting groups then at large.

However, this reliance placed upon the outmoded strategy – discredited in the First World War – of having cruisers patrol the trade routes with especial emphasis on focal points of merchant shipping, had yielded nothing. German commanders knew that if they struck trade routes at right angles and then withdrew at speed, rather than hitting the focal concentration-points, they would retain the initiative as long as it was possible to do so. Luck might play a part but then efficient lookouts and swift disengagement, combined with an almost religious refusal to engage a superior enemy force might win even that capricious lady's favour.

That said, the only advantage that lay with the Allies, and the British in particular, was the fact that time was not on the German side, demonstrated by the slow destruction of Germany's solitary and isolated merchant ships. Despite the best endeavours of Langsdorff and Dau, their supplies were finite and the Fatherland was distant. Now the time approached for the *Admiral Graf Spee* to make the best of her way home.

Against such a background – and his orders not to engage a superior force – Langsdorff's decision to make one last strike is surprising. That he wished to measure himself and his ship against an enemy force worthy of his steel is less so, given what we know of his career and character. However, in making a sudden descent upon the focal point off the Rio de la Plata, while it risked being intercepted by one of the hunting groups, carried long odds against that occurring precisely at the moment the *Admiral Graf Spee* fell upon any merchant ships there. After all, no molestations had taken place off the South American coast since the loss of the *Clement* weeks earlier and none at all as far south as the Rio de la Plata.

But the intelligence about the movements of the *Highland*

*Monarch*, the *Andalucia Star* and the small convoy with its naval escort, tempted Langsdorff into what was to seem like a well-laid trap. It was nothing of the kind, of course, and might well have miscarried, but the fact that while Langsdorff was guessing wrong another naval commander was guessing right, is the first indication that the initiative had changed hands.

Langsdorff was confident as he ordered his ship into action; after a brief hiatus in response to Wattenberg's cautionary advice he is reported to have responded, 'I suspect a convoy . . .' It would make, he concluded, 'a fine target'.

### British Cruiser Squadron (Force G)
### 2–12 December: 'The Plate . . . Was the Vital Area'
The man who guessed right was Commodore Henry Harwood, one of D'Oyly Lyon's divisional chiefs and the commander of Force G. This was an all-cruiser squadron consisting of HMSs *Exeter*, *Cumberland*, *Achilles* and *Ajax*, charged with protecting British interests in South American waters and – ever since the alarm had been raised – of seeking out any commerce raider attacking merchant shipping in the western South Atlantic.

At the outbreak of war *Ajax*, under Captain C.H. Woodhouse, had been the solitary occupant of the station, though nominally under the orders of Commodore Harwood in *Exeter*. On the very day that war broke out *Ajax* intercepted the 4,756-ton German merchantman *Olinda*, another German vessel belonging to the Hamburg-Südamerikanische Dampfschiffahrts Gesellschaft. The *Olinda*'s crew scuttled her under shellfire from *Ajax* without apparent loss of life. Shortly afterwards *Ajax* was joined by the heavy cruiser *Exeter*,

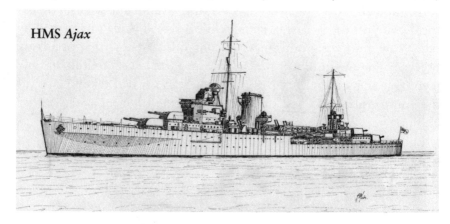

HMS *Ajax*

flying Commodore Harwood's broad pendant and commanded by Captain F.S. Bell. Following the general alarm raised by the Admiralty, *Ajax* had initially been sent to join Force K but had soon afterwards rejoined Harwood's squadron, which by late October had been augmented by the *Ajax*'s sister *Leander*-class ship, HMNZS *Achilles*. Although commanded by a regular British naval officer, Captain W.E. Parry, the *Achilles* was manned largely by New Zealanders, and she arrived in the Falkland Islands from New Zealand by way of the Southern Ocean, Valparaiso and the Straits of Magellan on 22 October. She joined *Exeter* on 26 October and Harwood put *Exeter* and *Achilles* through their paces in joint manoeuvres. Next day Harwood transferred his broad pendant to *Ajax* and sent *Exeter* south to Port Stanley in the Falkland Islands for a self-refit and boiler-clean, and to allow her crew a run ashore.

---

### CAPTAIN CHARLES HENRY WOODHOUSE
### of HMS *Ajax*

Charles Woodhouse was born in 1893 and educated at the Royal Naval Colleges of Osborne and Dartmouth. By the outbreak of the First World War he had been commissioned sub-lieutenant and was appointed to serve in HMS *Bristol*. In this cruiser he fought under Sturdee at the Battle of the Falkland Islands on 8 December 1914, when a British cruiser squadron annihilated a similar force under Admiral Maximilian Reichsgraf Von Spee.

Woodhouse was awarded a CB after the Battle of the River Plate and served in the Admiralty between 1940 and 1942 first as Deputy Director and then Director of the Local Defence Division. In 1942 he was appointed captain of the new battleship HMS *Howe*, a post he held until December 1943 before returning to the Admiralty. In 1946 he was promoted rear admiral and appointed to command the aircraft carriers and then the cruisers of the British Pacific Fleet. In 1948 he was made a vice admiral and appointed Commander-in-Chief of the East Indies, holding this post until his retirement in 1950, by which time he had been knighted. Although retired, he was made a full admiral in 1952.

## CAPTAIN WILLIAM EDWARD PARRY of
## HMNZS *Achilles*

Born in 1893, like his colleagues, Parry went to Osborne and Dartmouth before serving his time as midshipman. He passed for lieutenant with five first-class papers and served at sea throughout the First World War, only attending one shore course to specialize in torpedoes. He was promoted captain in 1934 and two years later commanded HMS *Osprey*, the Anti-Submarine Experimental Establishment at Portland until the following year, 1937. At this point Parry was 'loaned' to the New Zealand Division of the Royal Navy, precursor to the independent New Zealand Navy, a post he handled with great skill, assuming command of HMNZS *Achilles* in 1939. Like his fellow captains, Parry was made a CB for his part in Harwood's squadron. Back in New Zealand he became First Naval Member of the Royal New Zealand Navy Board and Chief of the Naval Staff.

In 1943 Parry returned to the Royal Navy to command the battlecruiser *Renown* and the following year hoisted his flag as a rear admiral, commanding Force L in Operation *NEPTUNE*, the naval element of the D-Day landings. Following the success of the invasion, Parry was appointed to the staff of the Allied Naval Commander of the Expeditionary Force and was stationed in Berlin after the end of the war.

In 1946 Parry served for two years as Director of Naval Intelligence and in 1948 was promoted vice admiral, whereupon he was 'loaned' again, relieving Admiral John Talbot Savignac Hall as Commander-in-Chief of the Indian Navy on 14 August 1948. His nominal flagship was the former *Achilles*, renamed *Delhi*. In October 1951 Parry reverted to the Royal Navy and was made a full admiral, finally retiring in 1952, having been knighted for his services.

Henry Harwood had been aboard the *Exeter* since his appointment in 1936 and he and the *Exeter* had spent their pre-war time in South

American waters. Initially he commanded the ship, later having a post-captain under him and hoisting his broad pendant as Commodore. He was a seasoned officer, having started his naval career at the age of fifteen. In 1906 he left the old training ship *Britannia* at Dartmouth top of his class and thirty years later was described as a 'sociable, clubby man who loved country sports'. At home he was devoted to his family of two young sons; at sea his enthusiasm for exercise and swimming might have his ship's company over the side for a swim, or toiling at one emergency drill after another. This tough but rational approach was timely, bringing his ship – and later those of his enlarged squadron – rapidly into a state of readiness for whatever the vicissitudes of war were to throw in their way. Their captain's enthusiasm for such energetic activity was not always shared by the older members of the lower deck.

**HMS *Achilles***

Harwood had also taken some thought for the future in larger, tactical matters. The emergence in the late 1930s of the German Navy as a possible enemy had, not unnaturally, focused the thoughts of British naval officers on the possibility of encountering what were then thought of, with a grudging admiration, as 'pocket battleships'. While serving at the Royal Naval College at Greenwich, Harwood had himself made a study of the *Kriegsmarine*'s new *Panzerschiff* as a potential commerce raider. In particular he had considered their effect at large on the South Atlantic and its pattern of sea-trading routes. Indeed, it had become something of an obsession, for in the summer of 1939, *Exeter* had been in New York for the World's Fair. Here Harwood's family recall he had seemed mesmerized by a large map showing the movements of merchant shipping in South American waters. To what extent other exhibits engaged Harwood's attention that day is uncertain, but with hindsight, the time he spent studying the concentration of shipping off the Rio de la Plata seems almost prescient. There had also been an occasion in 1937 when Harwood had visited Montevideo in *Exeter* and requested a joint exercise with the Uruguayan corvette *Huracan*. Her captain, *Capitán de Fragata* Varela, agreed to 'represent an enemy warship taking refuge in the River Plate', recorded Sir Eugen Millington-Drake, 'in order to gain better knowledge of navigating in the estuary [. . .] [This] is a characteristic example of Harwood's long preparation and intelligent anticipation'. It might also have been sheer fluke, but it bore out the old seafaring practice of 'forehandedness', of preparing for the worst eventuality while hoping for the best.

Forehanded or not, Harwood was well aware of the significance of such focal points in the area under his especial care as matters evolved in those early weeks of the war and the threat of German commerce raiding became a reality.

But it was not only the estuary of the Rio de la Plata that concerned Harwood. He had also to think of the approaches to Rio de Janeiro, to the adjacent choke-point off Cape Frio, and to the Falkland Islands, which, as the anniversary of the humiliation of the Imperial German Navy off that archipelago on 8 December approached, might be bombarded by an enemy raider. Having left *Cumberland* to patrol off the Rio de la Plata and *Achilles* off Rio de Janeiro, Langsdorff's depredations off the Cape of Good Hope had drawn Harwood in *Ajax* eastwards, but with no luck. Harwood now returned to the west, allowing *Ajax* a brief respite in Port Stanley. However, as the anniversary of Graf von Spee's defeat approached, he decided to relieve *Cumberland* off the Rio de la Plata with *Ajax* and send the heavy cruiser to join *Exeter* in the Falklands by the 7th December. If no threat materialized on or around the 8th, she was to go into Port Stanley and undergo a much-needed boiler-clean, whereupon *Exeter* was to rejoin Harwood.

With this plan in mind and the consequent movements in train, Harwood left Port Stanley in *Ajax* on 2 December and that same day he received the news of *Doric Star*'s sinking. Early next morning, before sunrise, he was also informed of another loss, that of the *Tairoa*, though the identity of the ship was then unknown to him. This intelligence came, as already noted, by relay from the *Port Chalmers*, which had picked up the RRR signals made by both vessels as they came under attack.

On the bridge of *Ajax*, Harwood drew a signal pad towards him and carried out an assessment. In his despatch after the action Harwood explained his decision-making process:

> The British ship *Doric Star* had reported being attacked by a pocket battleship in position 19° 15' South, [00]5° 5' East during the afternoon of 2nd December, 1939, and a similar report had been sent by an unknown vessel [in fact the *Tairoa*] 170 miles south-west of that position at 05.00 GMT on 3 December.
>
> From this data I estimated that at a cruising speed of 15 knots the raider could reach the Rio de Janeiro focal area a.m. 12th December, the River Plate focal area p.m. 12th December or a.m. 13th December and the Falklands Islands area 14th December.
>
> I decided that the Plate, with its larger number of ships and its very valuable grain and meat trade, was the vital area to be defended. I therefore arranged to concentrate there my available forces in advance of the time at which it was anticipated the raider might start operations in that area.

He kept the scrap of signal paper, afterwards even – as Eric Grove amusingly and touchingly records, given the outcome – 'having several copies of it made by an expert forger, hence the number of apparent "originals".'

But there were other details. In addition to this crucial assessment Harwood also considered the matter of logistics: first, the fuel oil available to him if compelled to linger off the Rio de la Plata then held in two chartered tankers, the Eagle Oil Company's *San Castro* and the *Capulet*, owned by a subsidiary of the Bowring Steamship Company, the Bear Creek Oil and Shipping Company; and second, the time and distance involved if a recall of the *Cumberland* became necessary.

Later that day, at 13.15 ship's time, having made his decision, Harwood signalled his squadron. On the face of it they were routine movements: *Achilles* was to leave Rio de Janeiro and proceed to Montevideo, where she was to refuel on the 8th; on completion of bunkering she was to steam to a rendezvous with Harwood in *Ajax* in Latitude 35° 00' South, Longitude 050° 00' West on the afternoon of the 10th; meanwhile *Cumberland* was to head south and proceed to the Falklands to commence her boiler-clean; on the 9th *Exeter* was to leave Port Stanley, steaming north to be off the Medanos lighthouse at 07.00 on the 12th. Having cast his net, thereafter the Commodore would issue further orders and until that time strict radio silence would be maintained by the squadron. This might have triggered alarm to any enemy interceptors if it had not been anything more than the prudent precautions taken by an experienced cruiser commander. The same might be said of the especial orders to the captain of HMS *Cumberland*. While undergoing her required boiler-clean and self-refit no more than half of her propulsion should be out of commission for anything other than a short period. In other words not all her boilers would be blown-down at the same time, an instruction in which it was implicit that she might be recalled at short notice.

As *Cumberland* steamed south and *Ajax* north, the two cruisers came in sight of each other and received an unexpected bonus. On 5 December they intercepted the German blockade runner *Ussukuma*, a 7,834-ton freighter belonging to the Hamburg-based Deutsche Ost-

# British Cruiser Squadron (Force G): 2–12 December

Afrika Linie, a company having interests associated with the Woermann Linie AG, which had already lost several ships to British cruisers. The *Ussukuma's* crew scuttled her. (Elsewhere, on the 9th, the *Shropshire* intercepted the blockade runner *Adolf Leonhardt*. She too was scuttled.) With *Cumberland* in the Falklands Commodore Harwood's 'available forces' made their rendezvous about 150 miles off the estuary of the Rio de la Plata as planned at about 06.00 on the forenoon of 12 December. Forming line-ahead they moved off to the south-eastwards, heading for a new position of Latitude 32° 00' South, Longitude 047° 00' West. At noon Harwood sent a signal by Aldis lamp to the *Exeter* and *Achilles* from *Ajax*, which made his intentions plain.

> My policy with three cruisers in company versus one pocket battleship. Attack at once by day or night. By day act as two units, First Division (*Ajax* and *Achilles*) and [Second Division] *Exeter* diverged to permit flank marking. First Division will concentrate gunfire . . .

Night dispositions were more complex, requiring an initiating signal from *Ajax*, whereupon the ships would turn onto a specific course to surprise the enemy, form up on the rear ship and cross the enemy's stern. In the event the night plan was unnecessary, but Harwood, with characteristic thoroughness, carried out a full manoeuvre exercise that evening after dark.

Harwood intended to fly off air reconnaissance next morning. Two Walrus amphibian aircraft were available aboard *Exeter*, but neither was in good condition. The Fairey Seafox aboard *Ajax* was operational and had been carrying out secret infra-red photo-reconnaissance flights over the Brazilian coast, seeking German U-boat bases. Although this experience had made the recovery team adept at lifting their seaplane back aboard, Harwood was taking no chances and decided to harbour his resources. He cancelled the routine dawn air patrol. The Seafox would be launched later in the morning. He could hardly have expected to find his enemy so soon.

## COMMODORE HENRY HARWOOD HARWOOD
### (19 January 1888–9 June 1950)

Henry Harwood Harwood was born in Suffolk on 19 January 1888, son of Surtees Harwood Harwood of Ashmans Hall. In 1903, at the age of fifteen, he joined the old *Britannia*, a static naval-training ship lying at anchor in the River Dart in Devon from which he passed out top of his class in 1906. He gained first-class passes in his examinations for lieutenant, specializing in torpedo warfare. This put him in the forefront of electrical technical development and he attended HMS *Vernon*, the Royal Navy's torpedo school at Portsmouth, and afterwards the Royal Naval College at Greenwich, long periods of training that occupied him between 1911 and 1913. During the First World War he served first as torpedo officer in the armoured cruiser *Sutlej* and then the battleship *Royal Sovereign*, part of the Grand Fleet's First Battle Squadron. By the end of the war he had been promoted to lieutenant commander.

In 1919 he joined the light cruiser *Southampton* in South American waters, taking the opportunity to learn Spanish and, when possible, travel up-country. After a brief period in the light cruiser *Dartmouth*, Harwood was promoted commander. Having attended the Staff Course back at Greenwich, he served in the Plans Division of the Naval Staff before being assigned to the Mediterranean Fleet. Here he rapidly rose to Fleet Torpedo Officer before being appointed Executive Officer to the new-building *Cumberland*, then undergoing construction at Barrow-in-Furness before being sent on her first commission to the Far East. He married in 1924, he and his wife having two sons before the outbreak of the Second World War.

At the end of 1928 Harwood was promoted to captain and was briefly in command of the destroyer *Warwick*, leader of the Fifth Destroyer Flotilla, leaving her in 1931. After attending the Imperial Defence College, Harwood was next appointed to command the cruiser *London*, which took him back to the crack Mediterranean Fleet. HMS *London* was flagship of the fleet's

Second Cruiser Squadron, and her captain was, *ex officio*, the squadron's chief staff officer, experience that led him back to Greenwich as a lecturer to the Senior Officer's War Course. Here, between 1934 and 1936 he was part of a team developing a new doctrine on divisional tactics arising from unsatisfactory elements in the conduct of the Grand Fleet during the First World War. In particular Harwood conducted a series of studies that included dealing with the new German *Panzerschiff* with her two heavy-calibre gun turrets. Despite the massed firepower available, herein lay the solution to engaging such a ship, for Harwood advocated an engagement in which a British force was divided in order to either compel the enemy to divide his firepower, or to concentrate it on one division at a time. By such means, believes Professor Grove, Harwood considered a theoretical disadvantage might be turned to a practical advantage. Harwood can, however, scarcely have dared hope he would be that *rara avis*, a theoretician who was called upon to demonstrate the validity of his argument in the white-heat of war.

In 1936 Harwood was appointed to HMS *Exeter*, a command that gave him a large measure of independence as the heavy cruiser was the senior ship in the South American Division of the Royal Navy's America and West Indies Station. Under his wing he had the light cruiser *Ajax* and at the time the appointment was one of 'showing the flag'. Consequently HMS *Exeter*, her captain and ship's company became familiar sights in Montevideo, establishing good relations with the Uruguayans, an endeavour to which Harwood bent all his enthusiasms and charm. As a Roman Catholic Harwood's faith, his knowledge of Spanish, his interest in country pursuits and the local area in general removed many of the prejudices that another British naval commander might have generated.

In August 1939 *Exeter* returned to Plymouth to pay-off at the end of her South American deployment, but the war loomed and the commission was extended; instead she returned to her South Atlantic station. However, with war imminent, Harwood was joined in *Exeter* by Captain F.S. Bell, who took over direct command of the ship, elevating Harwood to a Commodore, First Class. Afterwards Captain Bell, mindful of a significant German commercial community in the locality, wrote: 'There is no doubt whatever that the presence of *Exeter* and the innumerable friendships made by her officers and men in these [South American] States has in no small degree moulded their sentiment towards the [British] Nation.'

Professionally Harwood was impressive with his keen intelligence, his capacity for work, his staff experience, attention to detail and cool nerve. 'No one,' a contemporary officer recalled, 'could ever have wished for a more cheerful shipmate.' The lower-deck's opinion of him was more trenchant, grumbling

**13 December, Midnight–06.00: 'The Squadron Was in Position . . .'**

During the middle watch of Wednesday 13 December the three British cruisers ranged east-north-east, on a course of 060° True at a modest speed of 14 knots. *Ajax*, flying Harwood's commodore's broad pendant and commanded by Captain Charles Woodhouse, was in the van, followed by Captain William Parry's largely New Zealand manned *Achilles*. Bell's *Exeter*, tired, with a slightly defective propeller damaged in a refuelling operation, and with a ship's company overdue for leave, short of fresh vegetables and tobacco, brought up the rear. Although *Ajax* was his first command, Woodhouse had been in these waters before, having been a sub-lieutenant in the light cruiser *Bristol* when Sturdee fell upon Graf von Spee off the Falklands in December 1914. As a junior officer Bell too had seen action in the battleship *Canada* at Jutland, while Parry had been a torpedo specialist like Harwood. Following a period at the Imperial Defence College Parry had been selected to command one of the two cruisers of the Royal Navy's New Zealand Division.

Although lacking *Cumberland*, the squadron's second heavy cruiser mounting 8-inch guns, Harwood's force was less contemptible than is sometimes considered when pitted against the *Admiral Graf Spee*'s 11-inch main, and 5.9-inch secondary armaments. Evaluations at his incessant drills, complaining of the boredom inherent in extended patrols but grudgingly appreciative of his essential professional skill. According to Captain Woodhouse (who is quoted by Dudley Pope) newly appointed to his first command, HMS *Ajax*, Harwood 'had a gift for winning the confidence and esteem of all he met . . .' Unusually for a senior British naval officer of his generation he: 'Took endless trouble to explain to all those whose [. . .] co-operation would be required in [an] emergency the measures which he anticipated would be necessary.' In this he followed the precepts of Nelson.

In his encounter with Hans Langsdorff, Harwood was exactly the right man at exactly the right time and – most significantly – in exactly the right place.

of the firepower and rapidity of execution give the British a heavier margin by approximately one-quarter that of the German ship. Such comparisons are, to some extent, academic but, in seeking a battle at close quarters, Langsdorff was not playing to his strengths. While *Exeter*'s range finding was said to be dodgy at high speed, the German's high-resolution equipment was faultless. Much depended upon other factors, much upon luck.

At 04.50, as dawn approached the ships' companies of Harwood's squadron went to routine action stations, a heightened state of readiness than the cruising stations maintained during the night. There had been a short manoeuvring exercise at 05.20 when, Harwood afterwards stated in his *Report of Proceedings*, 'the Squadron was in position 34° 34' S., 49° 17' W'. A full calibre shoot was planned for later in the forenoon, but at 05.40 they stood down to Day Defence Stations, which meant only one gun in each turret was manned and steam pressure was reduced to save fuel. The off-duty men, as will all sailors given the opportunity, turned back into their hammocks for a short nap. Aerial reconnaissance might be cancelled, but some routines were as sacrosanct as they were sensibly precautionary. Nor were the old hands in the watches below going to miss the opportunity for a little more kip. They got 'about twenty minutes'.

## The *Admiral Graf Spee*
### 13 December, 06.00–06.17: 'Signalled for Identification'

At about 06.00 Langsdorff ordered his ship's engines worked up to full speed. Worn as they were the heavy diesels churned out the revolutions and as the speed climbed, so too did the complex harmonics throughout her hull. At 21 knots the vibration reached its climax, falling back as the speed rose to 24 knots. It did not disappear, however, and could be felt high up in the conning tower. As the fire-control system resolved the complex offset and elevation problems inherent in firing over a range of some 10 miles, the guns rose in response to this resolution. At this point the vibration affected a small screw in the electrical control motors driving the forward turret and *Fregattenkapitän* Ascher received the unwelcome news that his forward turret was affected. As the action opened, this 'could only fire when the ship turned to starboard to bring it on the target. The middle gun had to be disconnected to operate independently,' records Eric Grove, 'so that the turret could traverse.'

As the guns were being brought up to the firing position Langsdorff's signal ratings 'signalled the [British] warships for identification and ran up a masthead flag'. On the bridge Langsdorff now received two unwelcome reports: he learned about the fault to the forward turret. This was accompanied by the news that the two leading ships were not destroyers, but *Leander*-class light cruisers. He would also have noticed the absence of a convoy. To open the firing arc of his after guns and enhance his chances, Langsdorff altered course to 115° True (east-south-east), and ordered Ascher and his colleagues to engage. Then, Wattenberg recalled, Langsdorff 'betook himself, with the words "Now we will see!", to the foretop from which he conducted the action'. Other witnesses recorded he said: 'Let's do it.'

The *Admiral Graf Spee* opened fire at 06.17.

## British Cruiser Squadron (Force G)
### 13 December, 06.00–06.17: 'I Think It Is a Pocket Battleship'

As Langsdorff ordered the increase of speed that would rapidly decrease the range between the German ship and 'the convoy', the slight puff of yellow diesel exhaust emitted from the *Admiral Graf Spee*'s funnel rose in the crystal-clear morning air. It caught the eyes of two men on the bridge of *Ajax*. Leading Signalman Swanston saw and reported it, as did Lieutenant E.G.D. Lewin, *Ajax*'s Seafox pilot, who happened to be on watch.

Harwood and Woodhouse were informed, but ironically no one had yet identified the distinctive forebridge of the *Panzerschiff*. Their location suggested that the most likely sighting would be a British merchantman heading for what the British called the River Plate.

From the bunk in his sea cabin at 06.14 Harwood ordered a signal sent to Bell by lamp: 'Investigate smoke bearing 324 degrees . . .' He went on to tell Bell that if the stranger turned out to be a merchant ship he was to transfer a message to her for onward carriage to the British embassy at Montevideo, enabling the British ships to maintain radio silence.

The *Ajax*'s signalman had hardly got this signal under way when a string of coloured flags soared up *Exeter*'s flag halliards: 'Have sighted smoke bearing 320 degrees.' The heavy cruiser was already heeling as she turned to port, out of line, and began her detachment from Harwood's First Division. A moment later, at 06.16, her signal projector burst into life and informed the squadron with almost naïve enthusiasm, 'I think it is a pocket battleship.'

Lieutenant Commander C.J. Smith, HMS *Exeter*'s torpedo officer, now confirmed the identity of the strange vessel 'as a pocket battleship of the *Scheer*-class' and, as *Exeter* moved outwards from the two light cruisers' wakes, the signal N322 was run up, signifying an enemy in sight bearing 322° True. The same conclusion had occurred to those on *Ajax*'s bridge and a convinced Lewin hit the alarm buzzers, which rattled out the Morse letter 'A'. It was about 06.16.

Harwood grabbed a pair of uniform trousers and drew them over his pyjamas. Pulling on a reefer jacket he hurried to the bridge of *Ajax* as the Royal Marine bugler sounded off. Aboard *Achilles* the officer of the watch was joined by Captain Parry, both men lowered their binoculars and, turning to each other, eyes alight, exclaimed 'My God, it's a pocket battleship!'

# The Battle of the River Plate

The squadron was electrified; as the strident notes of the three ships' bugles echoed off the cold, grey, steel plates, the upperdeck men ran to their battle stations. Above their heads, in response to the tugging halliards of the signalmen, the three British cruisers ran up their large, conspicuous battle ensigns. Aboard *Achilles* the white ensign of the Royal Navy was run up the foremast, the naval ensign of New Zealand was worn at the truck of the mainmast. With the men at their action stations, the gunnery director swung and the guns followed, traversing and elevating onto the target. 'Four minutes only,' recalled Lieutenant Richard Washbourn, *Achilles*'s gunnery officer, 'though most of the sailors were enjoying their very necessary beauty sleep at the time and we were only at cruising stations. We were rather proud of that, even though *Exeter* beat us to it.'

Then at 06.17 the *Admiral Graf Spee* opened fire.

## The Battle of the River Plate: Morning Action
**13 December, 06.17–07.00: 'We Zigzagged Continually at High Speed . . .'**
Even before she pulled out of Harwood's line and began to close the range, the *Exeter* was the nearest target to Ascher's guns. She loomed large in the Zeiss optics as the rangefinders made her twin images merge and Ascher, high in the director tower, supervised the data as it was processed to offset and elevate the 28cm (11-inch) main armament. The *Korvettenkapitän*'s first ranging salvo was spread over about 380 metres and fell short; the second straddled the British cruiser. The third was closer still and began a punishing ordeal for the ship. It began with a near-miss on the *Exeter*'s starboard side, which detonated and sent splinters sweeping across the upper deck, killing several men at her starboard torpedo tube mounting and striking the amphibious Walrus 'Shag-bat' on that side. This was being prepared for launching, but as it now joined the other Walrus as being useless, both were hove overboard. Shell-splinters also knocked out the communications net's circuitry at the after control position and, entering the starboard flat through the cruiser's shell-plating, killed two men and pierced the hydraulic piping of the steering telemotor.

As Harwood reached the bridge of *Ajax* and took stock it seemed to him that the discharges from the *Admiral Graf Spee*'s after guns and the columns of water rising about the *Exeter* indicated the immediate success of his tactic: he had already divided Langsdorff's fire. At any second the forward turret would engage *Ajax* and *Achilles* as they maintained their course to the east-north-east, diverging from *Exeter*, but on a converging course with the German *Panzerschiff*. This did not happen, and even the rate of fire from Langsdorff's operational turret was slow: four salvoes in the opening five minutes.

*Korvettenkapitän* Ascher's opponent was Lieutenant Commander Richard Jennings, HMS *Exeter*'s gunnery officer. As his ship hauled out of line and headed to investigate the strange ship, Jennings's gun crew rapidly reported their turrets ready. As soon as Bell, with the *Admiral Graf Spee*'s ranging shot throwing up columns of water ahead of him, ordered fire returned, Jennings responded. The heavy cruiser's two forward turrets opened fire at 06.20 at a range of about 18,500 metres. Jennings also fired with a slow and concentrated deliberation, and he too achieved a straddle with the third salvo from A and B turrets' four guns. Captain Bell threw the speeding cruiser's helm over, adopting a shallow zigzag and opening the firing arcs of his after, X and Y turrets, but then the steering was knocked out with the severing of the telemotor's hydraulic pipework.

Nevertheless, by the sixth salvo Jennings's gunners scored themselves, hitting the *Admiral Graf Spee*. A shell struck a starboard 10.5cm (4.1-inch) anti-aircraft gun mounting and killed about half of the gun's crew before penetrating two decks and exploding in a workshop far below. The shell-burst destroyed the searchlight workshop, the ammunition hoist for the smashed anti-aircraft mounting above and the freshwater distilling plant. Simultaneously a shell near-missed, exploding alongside, a little abaft the forward turret; splinters penetrating the anti-torpedo blister and slicing into the ship's topside.

At about the same moment, around 06.20, aboard the *Admiral Graf Spee*, the offending screw had been found and replaced, bringing the forward turret back into action. Able now to overwhelm the approaching *Exeter*, Ascher began firing with six-gun broadsides from both turrets. With a high trajectory, one 28cm shell passed right through the entry hatch abaft *Exeter*'s B turret and into the sickbay below, before passing out of the ship through her port side without detonating; another hit the 1-inch armour of B turret. This was situated immediately ahead of, and just below *Exeter*'s open bridge and the shell – a nose-fused high explosive round – detonated on impact. The massive blast put the turret out of action and sent a shower of steel splinters sweeping over the cruiser's bridge. Only three men survived: Captain Bell and his torpedo and control firing officers, though Bell was wounded in the face. It also wrecked the communications system in the wheelhouse immediately below so that command and control of *Exeter* was now utterly compromised. Despite his wound, Bell immediately shifted to the after control position, only to find its communications severed and the ship was swinging round to starboard in a slow turn. Lieutenant Commander C.J. Smith, the Torpedo Officer, contacted the after steering position and ordered the firing arcs to be kept open and Bell, finding Midshipman Bonham at his station at the after control position, despatched him with further instructions. In only a few minutes *Exeter* was back under the wounded Bell's control again, a chain of men relaying helm orders from the after control position to the emergency after steering in a drill that, however well rehearsed under exercise conditions, actually worked efficiently under heavy enemy fire.

With flames flickering on her deck, the *Exeter* continued at full speed, heading west-north-west, firing doggedly from A and Y turrets, but getting no closer than a series of near-misses. All the time she was taking punishment from the *Admiral Graf Spee*'s first-rate optically controlled guns. Frequent exploding near-misses kept the upperdeck – with a string of vulnerable ratings passing Bell's helm orders exposed along a part of it – showered with shell fragments and causing grievous wounds, and 'two more 11-inch hits were received in the fore part of the ship during this phase'. Thus far Harwood's tactic had failed in part, for *Exeter* alone had attracted the *Panzerschiff*'s heavy-calibre armament.

As *Exeter* had turned to investigate and then engage, His Britannic Majesty's light cruisers *Ajax* and *Achilles* had held their course to the east-north-east. There was some relief aboard *Achilles* at a few moments peace, while Langsdorff impetuously 'covered the rather unpleasant stretch of water in which he could outrange us'. The British light cruisers were making 25 knots by about 06.21, when *Ajax* led round to port to close the range.

Within a few seconds, Langsdorff had also turned to port to avoid a torpedo attack by the two light cruisers and, for a few moments, both the *Admiral Graf Spee* and Harwood's division ran roughly parallel, the two British cruisers off the *Panzerschiff*'s starboard quarter. At about 06.22 *Achilles* opened fire, followed by *Ajax* and three minutes later, using radio signals between the two, a concentration of fire was achieved with *Ajax* directing. Unfortunately the plot misjudged the enemy's course and the two cruisers fired over their target.

*Korvettenkapitän* Kurt Meusemann was in charge of the *Admiral Graf Spee*'s 15cm (5.9-inch) secondary armament and he laid those on the starboard side upon the *Ajax* and *Achilles* alternately. 'He scored a pretty little straddle after twenty minutes,' *Achilles*'s gunnery officer wrote afterwards, 'his H[igh] E[xplosive shells] burst on the water and the pieces peppered us.' Meusemann's guns, Washbourn thought, 'weren't very effective'. However the *Achilles*'s second-in-command, Commander Mortimer Neame, recalled that splinters from these early salvoes carried away the halliards of the white ensign at the foremast-head, and thereafter, 'very significantly, considering that two-thirds of the ship's company were New Zealanders, we fought the action under this [i.e. the New Zealand] flag . . .'

At 06.26, Langsdorff had dismissed the threat of a torpedo attack and swung the *Admiral Graf Spee*'s head round to starboard, resuming his former heading of east-south-east. These two forces were now on converging courses.

At 06.28 the light cruisers' shells began to straddle the *Admiral Graf Spee*. With the *Exeter* showing signs of being on fire and with one turret inactive, Langsdorff ordered Ascher to shift target with the main armament onto the leading British light cruiser, HMS *Ajax*. As three salvoes straddled his flagship at 06.31, Harwood responded by edging away a little, to head north-north-east, open the range, and throw off the German rangefinders, still believing that he had successfully divided Langsdorff's fire. In fact Ascher was firing three-gun salvoes to find the new range.

In the brief respite this afforded the *Exeter*, much had been going on aboard the battered heavy cruiser. She was making water from splinter holes forward and water was being hosed into her from the fire-fighting parties dousing the conflagrations on the upper deck and the flats below. On the starboard side Lieutenant Commander Smith had mustered a party of torpedo ratings and had succeeded in restoring the firing circuits of the starboard mounting. Somewhere between 06.31 and 06.36, at an extreme range of around 13,000 yards, Smith set his Mark VII torpedoes and unleashed them.

It was at this point that Langsdorff, concerned that Harwood would cross ahead of him, began to swing to port. The manoeuvre that had reduced his silhouette and deceived so many innocent and unsuspecting merchant officers – an approach end-on – would mask his after turret while exposing his ship to all sixteen of Harwood's guns. How close along the *Admiral Graf Spee*'s side Smith's torpedoes ran, or where they exploded at the end of their run, remains a mystery, for Langsdorff turned out of their path and no one aboard the *Panzerschiff* was aware than the battered *Exeter* had attempted so bold a move.

At 06.36, as he turned his ship away from Harwood, Langsdorff again shifted target, re-engaging the *Exeter* in a deadly action as she moved clear of her own smoke. As the heavy-calibre shells again rained down upon his ship, Bell fired back and Smith prepared his port torpedo tubes. When he was ready, Bell ordered the *Exeter* turned to starboard, towards Harwood in the distance and onto an approximately reciprocal course to Langsdorff. Harwood himself was also completing a turn to port by 06.36, heading about north-east to close the range, but Langsdorff now commenced his own port turn and made smoke.

Amid the shells from the guns of *Exeter*'s extreme forward and only after turret, there were several near-misses, at least one of which detonated and drove splinters into the *Admiral Graf Spee*'s port side as she turned. But, seeing the *Admiral Graf Spee* now heading a little north of west, Bell put his own helm over and *Exeter* followed the heavy German ship round so that at about 06.48 both were now heading on roughly parallel courses, zigzagging along a median rhumb-line to confuse their opponent's range-finding.

Surprisingly *Exeter* now scored two more hits upon the *Panzerschiff*. One shell passed through the foretower and exploded in an air-burst on the starboard side of the ship. Langsdorff had by now realized what he was up against but preserved an admirable sang-froid: 'He said dryly and without taking his pipe out of the corner of his mouth: "We'll smash them" . . .' But in the lightly armoured foretop Langsdorff was exposed and was twice lightly wounded from this first shell-burst, 'in the shoulder and in the arm'. Later the blast from an exploding shell knocked him down and rendered him briefly unconscious. The second shell drove through the armoured belt amidships, only a little forward of the engine room, passed through an armoured bulkhead and exploded in another workshop. Several ratings were killed and, significantly, electrical cabling linking Ascher's fire-control director with the guns was severed.

This might have proved more dangerous had Bell not opted to turn *Exeter* hard a-starboard, in order to launch Smith's torpedoes from the port mounting. As *Exeter* turned, one of the *Admiral Graf Spee*'s 28cm shells struck A turret and disabled it: Bell had now lost all his forward guns and although the port torpedoes were fired, they missed. At this moment the *Admiral Graf Spee* hit her twice more with her heavy-calibre guns at a range of no more than 6 miles, the consequences of which were serious. The impact and detonation of the two shells was so near simultaneous that the entire ship shook with the powerful forces to which her fabric was subjected. One shell, having passed through the navigating officer's cabin in the forward superstructure, continued through the block and out of the far, starboard side, only to detonate on the barrel of the forward 4-inch high-angle anti-aircraft gun. A number of seamen were killed outright, others were wounded and the 4-inch ready-use ammunition was countermined and began exploding with splinters flying about in all directions. The second shell struck a little forward of the armoured belting and drilled through three bulkheads to detonate in the Chief Petty Officers' flat, above the anti-aircraft guns' magazine. Fortunately the armoured deck prevented the ammunition stowed below from going off, but fires ignited by the explosion looked fair to finish the job. Not only was the 4-inch magazine threatened, but so too were the magazine supplying B turret with 8-inch shells and charges, and the Walrus' bomb store. With the eighteen men stationed in the Chiefs' flat killed instantly and a major fire burning in the adjacent pantry, a Royal Marine sergeant, George Puddifoot, and an Engine Room Artificer, Frank Bond, decided to flood the 8-inch magazine. This trapped a number of men in the electrical power compartments and a rescue squad was assembled from a fire party.

This was not the end of *Exeter*'s woes, for splinter damage had cut the power supply to the Transmitting Station, which fed the fire-control commands to elevate and traverse the remaining turret aft. This was evacuated and Lieutenant Commander Jennings gave up his position and headed aft to take post on the after searchlight platform and attempt to regulate the heavy cruiser's last guns, which were now reduced to firing by eye in local control. This was rudimentary stuff, but not quite as primitive as Bell's conning had become.

In addition to the loss of his steering, forward armament and fire-control, poor Bell had also lost his gyro compasses through power failure. He was reduced to sending for a small magnetic boat-compass. But he still engaged his heavier enemy, now on the *Exeter*'s starboard beam, as each ship headed roughly west on slightly diverging courses and opening their distance from 6 miles. It was now about 06.55.

To the east an anxious Harwood had followed the *Admiral Graf Spee* as she turned to port. For a little while *Ajax* led *Achilles* north and then, as Langsdorff re-engaged Bell with his main armament at about 06.46, Harwood gradually swung to port, with slight variations of course to keep his after guns firing so that at 06.56 the two light cruisers were in hot pursuit of the *Admiral Graf Spee*, which was about 8.75 miles ahead of them, heading westwards with *Exeter* abaft her port beam but, as noted above, on approximately the same course.

Prior to the duel between Ascher's big guns and the *Exeter*,

Harwood's division had had trouble getting on target as they headed north-east. Analysis suggests that the *Admiral Graf Spee*'s speed of advance and course were wrongly assessed and the turn she made to port *away* from the *Ajax* and *Achilles* – which was followed by a large and then lesser zigzags – went unobserved or was wrongly interpreted for a few moments, as the grey silhouette changed its aspect. It was not until *after* 06.36 before it became clear to Harwood's gunnery officers, led by Lieutenant D. Dreyer aboard *Ajax*, that Langsdorff had swung away obscured by his own smokescreen. This accumulation of errors and mischance threw the calculations of the fire-controller out. But by increasing to 28 knots and firing over the target, speed-input and gun elevation were reduced to retune the system. By using a sequence of shortening ranges and reductions in target speed to a better proximation of the 24 knots that the *Admiral Graf Spee* was actually making, the British gunnery improved. In the meantime, Harwood had ordered the *Ajax*'s Fairey Seafox airborne to 'spot' for the squadron.

This was not before time: Langsdorff's turn and subsequent zigzagging had enabled Meusemann to again lay his secondary armament on Harwood's ships to better effect. At 06.37, the point at which Langsdorff had completed his westwards turn and was zigzagging, and Bell was completing his starboard swing to fire his port torpedo tubes, Harwood hoisted the signal for an increase of squadron speed to 28 knots and led onto a roughly northerly course, which he held until 06.46 when, with Bell swinging *Exeter* to port to run parallel to Langsdorff, he brought his own division round to head west in pursuit of Langsdorff.

During this ten-minute period of uncertainty, as the *Ajax*'s gunners wrestled with the problem of getting back on target and an anxious Woodhouse did not wish to interrupt the process, Lieutenant Edgar Lewin had been launched by catapult between salvoes as *Ajax*'s gun blazed away. It was a disappointment that this 'very fine evolution' – which had required some nicely judged co-ordination to avoid Lewin's seaplane from being destroyed by the blast from *Ajax*'s guns – was now compromised by another failure. On the catapult, awaiting the right moment to go, the Seafox's observer, Lieutenant R. Kearney had signalled to the deck that he would retain the reconnaissance frequency of 230kHz and not switch to the 3,800kHz used for spotting. This would, he thought, save time. Alas, it had the contrary effect, for the message failed to reach the wireless operators and it took twelve minutes for the operators to twig what had happened.

Although Dreyer, still controlling both light cruisers' gunnery 'as one', had not only closed the range but had hit the enemy, having turned and zigzagged, the *Admiral Graf Spee* also emitted dark and billowing clouds of smoke. Despite this obscurity, Dreyer's hits were telling and although *Exeter* had damaged the enemy's forward rangefinder, there was nothing wrong with the after one, from which Ascher now focused on Harwood's pursuing division. A near-miss had a devastating effect upon *Achilles* and her young and hitherto untried crew. One shower of splinters killed three ratings at a forward anti-aircraft gun, another swept the bridge, shattering the knee of Chief Yeoman Martinson and wounding Captain Parry in both legs. 'Our captain acquired a sizish hole in both legs,' wrote Washbourn, sitting above in the rotating fire-director control tower. This was trained to port and now Washbourn and his men 'had rather more than our share,' as he told a friend later. After 'a hideous clang and a fairly heavy concussion', six shell splinters 'came inside. With my usual fantastic luck three pieces impinged on my ample anatomy [. . .] but caused me little inconvenience, apart from a certain mental vagueness of the ensuing minute or two'.

The shell splinters had entered the starboard side. Inside it was 'a shambles'. Two telegraphists 'were inert bloodstained bundles of serge', one of the rangefinding operators had fallen on the Royal Marine spotter with 'nauseating wounds in the face and thighs'. This man, Able Seaman E.V. Shirley, 'quietly applied a tourniquet to himself and saved his life thereby,' while the spotter underneath 'had lost large portions of both buttocks but he, most gallantly, said nothing at the time and stuck it out'. Washbourn did not discover Sergeant Trimble was wounded 'until the first lull about an hour later, when he nearly fainted from loss of blood'. Another rating, an able seaman who operated the Range to Elevation and Deflection Unit had also been killed, unnoticed for some moments by Washbourn, who was actually wounded in the head. With blood pouring down his face, Washbourn continued

> to fire for some minutes with a dead man resting quietly in a very natural position against his instrument. This threw out our fire for some time which was a pity. When I did spot it, I ordered a young Ordinary Seaman across from the inclinometer. He couldn't get rid of his predecessor's mutilated body so he calmly sat down upon this unpleasantness and worked the instrument for the remaining hour of the action. Five out of the ten of us were out, three for keeps, and others took over quietly and did their stuff like absolute veterans, unmoved by the carnage among them.

In another letter Washbourn said of the young Ordinary Seaman that 'he had been a little wide-eyed after we had disengaged but was otherwise unmoved', adding: 'A splinter had jammed the door and prevented the medical parties from reaching us. The wounded never murmured.'

At 06.46, as both the *Admiral Graf Spee* and the *Ajax* and *Achilles* steadied on west-north-westerly courses, the two divisions had been about 8.5 miles apart, almost due east and west of one another. At this time the *Exeter*, beginning her swing to port to run west parallel to her heavy adversary, had been 6 miles south of the *Admiral Graf Spee*. At 06.56 the German ship altered course to the west, leaving *Exeter*'s bearing opening abaft her port beam, while Harwood – now about 7.8 miles on the *Panzerschiff*'s starboard quarter – pulled away to the north-west at full speed, opening the range slightly, but also opening his gun arcs as his gunners tried to hit the enemy in spite of the dense smoke the *Admiral Graf Spee* was making.

It was now 07.00. The engagement had, thus far, lasted a little over forty minutes.

During this phase the British Merchant Navy masters and officers held captive aboard the *Admiral Graf Spee* had had an anxious time. They had already noted the extreme youth of the bulk of Langsdorff's crew and one had, in conversation with

Langsdorff, remarked that a seaman was coiling a line the wrong way. Such a basic transgression of seamanship was indicative. Langsdorff admitted that his crew were mostly 'baker's boys' and the like. At about 06.00 that morning it was the urgency of the running footsteps of these young men that alerted the prisoners that something unusual was up.

Initial enthusiasm at an encounter with warships of the Royal Navy was quickly muted by contemplation of the appalling position these men were in. Several, among them Captain Pottinger of the *Ashlea*, thought the best antidote was routine, and they went for a shave. In due course Captain Patrick Dove and Radio Officer B.C. McCorry of the *Huntsman*, both tall men, were able to spy through the two tapped holes from which had been removed the bolts holding the plate denominating their prison the midshipmens' quarters. From here all that could be seen was relayed to the tense group of men waiting in the space behind them. Their greatest anxiety was for the three wounded boys who 'were still pretty groggy' and 'could only just crawl about [. . .] they were still in pain from the shell splinters embedded in their wounds'.

Pottinger remembered the

> repeated concussions [. . .] of big guns. We could not tell if these were the guns being fired by us or shells striking us. We zigzagged continually at high speed and heeled over so much that at times I thought we were going to capsize [. . .] We could see some men working at an ammunition hoist. They all looked very anxious. From what we could tell, things were not going too well with them. The dead were being piled up outside and the stench was awful. We could see men with rubber gloves on washing down the corpses with hoses . . .

Observers on the British cruisers remarked upon the agility with which this great ship answered her helm, 'like a ship half her size', one commented. But this did not secure her from *Exeter*'s guns and she was hit very quickly after opening fire. According to the testimony of Captain Dove,

There came an ear-splitting crash on the steel deck directly over our heads. All the lights went out [. . .] pieces of twisted steel and other debris showered all round us, and suddenly a stream of daylight broke through one corner of our prison [. . .] Through a fog of dust I saw everyone scatter [. . .] Some men picked up life jackets [. . .] for protection [. . .] others ducked under the tables. The wounded lad who could not move [. . .] was dragged under a table, and piles of hammocks were heaped over the top like a bombproof shelter.

Dust, debris, and the smell of explosive choked us. It was a long while before any of us ventured to move from our funkholes. From where I was crouching I could see the havoc the shell had wrought. There was a gaping hole where the deck had been split, but luckily the shell had struck the 6-inch angle beam of the half-inch steel deckhead above us. Had it struck the plating between the beams [. . .] It would have come through and burst among us [. . .] only large splinters had torn their way into our quarters. Yet by the most unlucky coincidence the only person to be wounded was the young lad who was already injured, and had been put under the table for safety. A splinter had gashed his arm [. . .] Now we could see [. . .] what was going on [. . .] Through the gash we could see the blue sky and also [. . .] the sea [. . .] It was blue and calm as a mill pond, and the thought at once passed through our minds that [. . .] we might at least have a chance of swimming for our lives.

Better still, we could tell from the position of the sun that the *Graf Spee* was steering in a westerly direction, and from the huge bow waves and the throb of the engines that she was flat out. All the guns we could see were trained aft [. . .] the *Graf Spee* was on the run, she was being chased!

Radio Officer McCorry 'felt very proud of the behaviour of my fellow Merchant Navy officer prisoners in the *Graf Spee*. Looking back on what I felt and did during that memorable battle I can see that it was the courage and bearing of my fellow officers which inspired me to give my best in return.'

**13 December, 07.00–08.00: 'She Looked Vicious and Efficient'**
Thus far Captain Bell's *Exeter* had taken the brunt of the *Admiral Graf Spee*'s venom.

Although by now virtually out of the action, *Exeter*'s gunnery had surprised the Germans and placed the *Panzerschiff* 'in great danger'. The effect of her shells, in piercing the *Admiral Graf Spee*'s armour had 'upset the view that she could only be successfully fought by a battleship'. Rasenack went on to say that the Germans 'underestimated the armour' of the *Exeter*. No armour-piercing shells had been used against her, 'which was fortunate for her. With eight hits, had they been armour-piercing shells, she would have been blown up.'

But by 07.00 the *Exeter* was no longer a viable fighting unit. She was heavily down by the head owing to sea water flooding into her forward compartments. The amount of water, estimated at some 650 tons, also caused her to list to starboard about 10 degrees. Her two forward turrets were out of action and her single after one, Y turret, was only capable of firing in local control under Chief Ordnance Artificer William Johns, owing to the entire gunnery control system and, of course, the navigating bridge and wheelhouse, being out of

---

**CAPTAIN F. S. BELL**
**of HMS *EXETER***
Captain F.S. Bell joined the Royal Navy after being educated at Matfield Grange between 1904 and 1910, going first to the Royal Naval College at Osborne, on the Isle of Wight, and then to Dartmouth. He served in HMS *Cumberland*, a predecessor of the cruiser then at Port Stanley, and in the Cameroons Campaign in the first year of the First World War. His next posting was to the battleship *Canada*, in which he fought at Jutland in 1916, before volunteering for submarines, in which he served until 1923. Various postings followed until his promotion to Commander in 1931, soon after which he was appointed to the Royal Naval Staff College at Greenwich. Two years later, in 1935, he was the Executive Officer of the battlecruiser HMS *Repulse*, leaving her when appointed post-captain in 1938. His

---

action. Only one of *Exeter*'s secondary 4-inch guns remained useful, both Walrus flying boats had been ditched, all internal telephone networks were down, and her radio system was shot to pieces. There were serious fires raging in the Chief Petty Officers' and servery flats and lesser fires on the Royal Marines' mess-deck and in the paint shop.

On the other hand the concentration of fire upon her forepart had left her engine and boiler rooms unscathed, unless one counts the superheat in the boilers, which had melted the brickwork within. With the ship listing, this had run over to starboard, and this was not the only consequence of the list: it made even routine duties difficult – a circumstance augmented by further shell-bursts and flying splinters – while it made matters difficult for both the wounded and the ministering sick berth parties, and especially so for Surgeon Lieutenant Lancashire, to whom many looked for survival.

For a little longer she fought on, listing and down by the head, as her enemy headed west, drawing away from her. From the control position in Y turret the *Admiral Graf Spee* could be clearly seen about

appointment to *Exeter* was, as noted in the main text, shortly before the outbreak of war in 1939.

After the Battle of the River Plate, Bell was appointed Flag Captain and Chief Staff Officer to the Flag Officer, Malaya, and as such was in Singapore on the eve of its fall and surrender to the Japanese. Captain Bell escaped, crossing the Malacca Strait in a yacht and, landing in Sumatera, made his way south to Padang by lorry and riverboat. He was embarked from Padang by a British warship, which landed him on the south coast of Java. From here he obtained a passage to Fremantle by a merchantman and rejoined the Royal Navy, being posted to command the battleship *Anson* in 1945, serving in the Pacific Ocean until bringing her home in 1946. He had contracted tuberculosis during his active service and was retired unfit in 1947, being appointed ADC to HM King George VI.

4.5 miles away, flying an enormous *Swastika*-emblazoned ensign. 'She looked vicious and efficient,' William Johns recalled, 'and as we fired at each other she stood out clear cut against the blue water on this lovely sunlit morning.'

Then, at 07.29 the electrical power supply to Y turret failed and *Exeter*'s last 8-inch guns fell silent. The *Admiral Graf Spee*'s near-misses, as she sped away, had caused splinter damage, which blew a hole in the *Exeter*'s side, allowing water in to short the power circuits to the after turret.

Bell was already making smoke to hide his wounded ship and at about 07.15 Ascher gave up laying his guns on her as she faded in the murk, 'no longer serviceable as a fighting unit'.

### The Battle of the River Plate: Chase to the West
### 13 December, 07.00–08.06: 'On Course for the River Plate'

The alteration of course to the westwards in pursuit of the *Admiral Graf Spee* by Harwood's division gave the gunnery teams in the British light cruisers problems. The smokescreen laid by the German warship was effective, though as Chief Petty Officer W.G. Boniface, *Achilles*'s Direct Control Tower Rangefinder, recalled 'her top rangefinder was nearly always visible'. Unfortunately, however: 'A good bit of vibration was set up inside our R/F by our speed and gunfire . . .'

At 07.08 Harwood decided to remedy this and altered course to port, losing A arcs 'in order to close the range as rapidly as possible [. . .] and *Ajax* and *Achilles* were ordered to proceed at their utmost speed'. The two light cruisers were now heading south of due west with only their forward guns able to bear upon the target, which was emitting the clouds of smoke foiling the British gunlayers. Nevertheless they were obliged to avoid the fall of shot from Langsdorff's 28cm guns by 'frequent violent alterations of course', usually towards the columns thrown up by the last shells.

Then, at 07.16, the *Admiral Graf Spee* 'made a drastic alteration to port under cover of smoke but four minutes later she turned to the north-west' under full helm, and in such a manner as to alarm Captain Pottinger, but which uncovered both her forward and after turrets upon the pursuers. '*Ajax* was immediately straddled three times,' though her secondary armament 'was firing raggedly [. . .] between *Ajax* and *Achilles*.' During the sudden turn she had also attempted to loose a spread of torpedoes, though only one was fired as the ship's swing threw the aiming out.

Harwood's response was to alter to starboard, make smoke and, opening all arcs, return fire at a range of about 5 miles. With all guns bearing the two cruisers' 'shooting appeared to be very effective, and a fire was observed amidships in *Graf Spee*'. Then, at 07.25 the *Ajax* suffered a direct hit from the *Admiral Graf Spee*'s main armament with a delayed action shell. This passed through the after part of the ship and ultimately destroyed the trunking below X turret and finally exploded in Harwood's accommodation. A section of the shell casing hit Y barbette, damaging the training rack and jamming the turret so that it could not traverse. Not only were both X and Y guns eliminated, but four men were killed and six wounded in the shell-burst. Two lighter calibre shells had hit *Ajax*'s bridge and her topmast fell.

Harwood immediately concluded that Langsdorff had abandoned the wounded *Exeter* and, by heading north-west and converging with his own line of advance, intended closing the range with the light cruisers. Harwood now decided that he must use his ship like the destroyers Langsdorff had at first taken them for and gave orders to prepare a broadside of torpedoes to be fired from *Ajax*.

Ordering Woodhouse to put the helm over, *Ajax* turned to starboard at 07.24 and fired her torpedoes, swinging back to port once they were running. Unlike Smith's from *Exeter*, *Ajax*'s torpedoes were seen and the *Admiral Graf Spee* again put her own helm hard over, turning 'some 130 degrees to port' and successfully evading the attack, though Langsdorff afterwards remarked how close they had been. Three minutes later 'she came back to the north-west'.

Ascher was now having considerable difficulties. The *Admiral Graf Spee* 'had suffered several more hits from the rapid fire of the cruisers, particularly *Achilles*', while her 'own gunnery had suffered through her alterations of course, the spotting difficulties, the handicap of having to engage targets that were well abaft the beam, interference to her secondary armament caused by her main armament and the failure of the after ammunition supply for her secondary armament. In consequence the achievements of *Spee*'s guns in the "following" action were poor'.

One of the shells was witnessed by Captain Dove:

> I saw a two-seconds scene that will be vivid in my memory till the day I die. I had a brief glimpse of men of the Number Three Port Gun crew handling shells into the breach of their 5.9-gun, then a shell [. . .] burst right on it.
>
> One moment there was a gun about to be fired and men working round it. Then there came a blinding flash and an explosion which sent me reeling [. . .] When I climbed up and looked again, the gun's crew had vanished. The gun [. . .] lay [. . .] on its side [. . .] That same shell smashed the jib of the electric crane on the port side and shattered the launch stowed on the skids under it [. . .] Look[ing] forward along the port side [. . .] was just one huge litter of wreckage [. . .] strewn everywhere.

During this phase of the action, despite the zigzagging, Harwood's cruisers had closed the range and turned generally to port, as though to cross the *Admiral Graf Spee*'s stern. At 07.31 Harwood had received a report from Kearney high above in the Seafox and at last in radio contact, that a spread of torpedoes appeared to have been fired, but that they would pass ahead. This seems to be an observational error – perhaps it was a school of dolphins – but it persuaded Harwood 'not to take any chances'. He steered south, 'engaging the enemy on the starboard side with the range closing rapidly'.

Langsdorff altered to south-west 'and again brought all guns to bear' upon *Ajax* and *Achilles*. While this closed the range still further, Harwood now received a worrying report: '*Ajax* had only 20 per cent of ammunition left'. With 'only three guns in action, as one of the hoists had failed in B turret and X and Y turrets were both out of action' and with '*Graf Spee*'s shooting [. . .] [apparently] still very accurate . . .' Harwood made up his mind. At 07.38, with the *Admiral Graf Spee* racing west, Harwood decided to break off the action and, trailing a smokescreen *Ajax* led *Achilles* round to a course of east. He intended 'to close in again after dark', but the enemy, Harwood thought, 'did not appear to have suffered much damage'.

At approximately the same time Captain Bell also came to a decision. He could no longer keep in the fight and had lost sixty-one men killed and twenty-three seriously wounded. It was about 07.40 when *Exeter* turned south and began to head for the Falklands and the refuge of Port Stanley.

As Harwood digested the consequences of the last hour and three-quarters he was aware that the *Admiral Graf Spee* 'made no attempt to follow the two British cruisers' but had steadied again on a due westerly course and at 22 knots was heading 'on a course direct for the River Plate'. A little later the depressing news of *Ajax*'s lack of ammunition was clarified. It referred only to A turret, though this was the only one capable of firing. Nevertheless, the worm of doubt uncoiled in Harwood's mind. Langsdorff, despite not appearing to have suffered much damage was not coming after his retreating cruisers; he was retreating himself. 'After opening the range under smoke for six minutes', by which time they were now almost 15 miles apart, Harwood resolutely threw his squadron back into action: 'I again turned the First Division to the westward . . .' ordering the two cruisers' courses to diverge so that *Achilles* took station on the enemy's starboard quarter, while *Ajax* took post upon her port.

Langsdorff now bent his course to west-south-west but: 'His very conspicuous control tower made it an easy matter to shadow him at long range in the visibility prevailing.'

It was 08.06.

## 13 December, 08.06–19.15: 'No Prospect of Shaking Off the Shadowers'

It was now time for Harwood to consider the greater picture, to shift from the tactical to the strategic. With *Ajax*'s aerials disabled and their replacement not yet aloft, he ordered *Achilles* to broadcast the *Admiral Graf Spee*'s position, course and speed to all British merchant ships. Once his own wireless transmitters were able to work again *Ajax* broadcast a revised but similar message 'every hour until the end of the chase'. The information was also sent to the Admiralty in London at 10.17 and 17.00. Meanwhile there were other matters to consider.

First there was *Exeter*: Harwood was uncertain of her condition. Shortly before *Ajax*'s aerials had been cut down, he had signalled Bell to join him, but had received no reply. Radio communications between the two cruisers then failed completely in both ships. In the end Harwood ordered Lewin launched in the Seafox with the order that Bell should close the commodore but Lewin, having located *Exeter*, reported her a shambles and returned to *Ajax*.

Leaving Woodhouse to break off the chase briefly to recover Lewin and Kearney in their Seafox at 09.12, Harwood next sent a signal recalling *Cumberland* from her boiler-clean at 09.46. This was corrupted and effectively undecypherable on receipt, but Captain W.H.G. Fallowfield guessed its content and its import. He immediately gave orders to clear *Cumberland* for sailing, getting under weigh at 10.00, and was well on his way when a repetition of the signal some hours later confirmed the rightness of his initiative. (As a consequence of his decision the *Cumberland* was off the Rio de la Plata within thirty-four hours, replacing the battered *Exeter*, and while she did not bring up the strength of Harwood's squadron to the proportions being propagated by Churchill's disinformation campaign, the presence of *Cumberland* had a powerful moral effect and was certainly magnified by the distant and anxious German observers aboard the *Admiral Graf Spee*.)

Harwood remained troubled by Bell's situation in *Exeter* but he was interrupted at 10.05 when the *Admiral Graf Spee*, observing the *Achilles* – now some way ahead of her consort – had closed the range to 11 miles, fired two, three-gun salvoes. One landed short, but observing this, Ascher corrected the settings and the second 'fell close alongside' the *Achilles*. Parry turned away under smoke, resuming his westwards course, when he observed Langsdorff to have done the same at an extended distance.

A little later, at 11.04, a steam tramp was seen close to the *Admiral Graf Spee* and a radio signal was received from the German ship addressed to *Ajax* to the effect that she should 'please pick up lifeboats of English steamer'. However, when the *Ajax* came up with the tramp, the S.S. *Shakespear* (*sic*), she reported herself unharmed, and the cruisers swept past her. [The *Shakespear* was sunk in January 1941 by the Italian submarine *Commandante Cappellini*.] At noon, with both *Ajax* and *Exeter* back on the air, an exchange of messages took place. Harwood now received a situation report from Bell. Apart from the battle damage to her armament, communications and steering, *Exeter* was now badly flooded forward but was capable in slight sea conditions of making 18 knots. Harwood confirmed Bell's intention of heading towards the Falklands, though an offer had been received from the Argentine Minister of Marine that he might bring *Exeter* into the Argentine naval base at Puerto Militar, close to Bahía Blanca. The consequences of this would have meant the internment for the duration of the war of any wounded men landed for medical treatment, and the revelation of the extent of the damage done to *Exeter*. Bell was anxious to avoid both outcomes, courteously declining this offer and headed for Port Stanley, distant 1,000 miles and lying in higher and stormier latitudes.

Harwood, meanwhile, informed the British Naval Attaché at Buenos Aires that the *Admiral Graf Spee* was heading for the Rio de la Plata after being in action with his squadron.

It seemed 'unimaginable' to many of the observers in the pursuing British cruisers that the *Admiral Graf Spee* – 'this fine ship' as Washbourn called her – 'with at least one 11-inch turret and one 5.9 in action, and almost her full speed, should be belting from one and a half small 6-inch cruisers both almost out of ammunition. We thought she must have something up her sleeve, and we watched eagerly for the next development.'

The anxiety of Washbourn and many others seemed confirmed at 15.43 when a signal for an 'enemy in sight' to the west-north-west broke out from *Achilles*'s flag halliards. All eyes trained to the starboard bow where, in the clear air, a superstructure was breaking the horizon. Was Langsdorff falling back on support? It seemed so as reports claimed that it was the upperworks of a *Hipper*-class heavy cruiser that was appearing over the rim of the world. It smacked of German efficiency, a clever move that somehow trumped the ace of

Harwood's foresightedness. On the two bridges there was no doubt about it and, for sixteen minutes success turned to ashes as they contemplated their fate. Then *Achilles* 'negatived the report' as 'the unmistakable fo'c's'le of a merchant ship rose above the horizon'. The strange ship was the almost brand-new British Lamport and Holt cargo liner *Delane* bound for Montevideo. The newfangled streamlining of her superstructure had fooled the anxious naval observers. 'Reprieve came as an anticlimax,' Washbourn confessed, such was their heightened state of mind.

That afternoon, falling far astern, her list uncorrected, the *Exeter* headed south. At 15.45 many of the ship's company mustered on the quarterdeck to bury the dead. Grimy, in tatterdemalion uniforms from the early summons to battle, they intoned the naval prayer, sang the naval hymn, *Eternal Father Strong to Save* . . . and committed the bodies of their fallen shipmates to their unmarked graves beneath the blue waters of the South Atlantic. In *Ajax* and *Achilles* similar short but moving services were held as the two cruisers followed their enemy.

As the sun westered Langsdorff's intentions became clear: he was definitely intending to enter the great estuary of the Rio de la Plata and at 18.00 the coast of Uruguay was in sight.

Throughout the forenoon and afternoon of that day the *Admiral Graf Spee* had raced west. During his withdrawal Langsdorff had licked his wounds and reviewed the condition of his ship and her young company. The *Admiral Graf Spee* had received two direct 8-inch shell hits from *Exeter* and eighteen 6-inch hits from *Ajax* and *Achilles*. This had destroyed all the galleys and wrecked the flour store. Hits forward had impaired her buoyancy and 'rendered her unseaworthy for the North Atlantic winter. One shell had penetrated the armour belt and the armoured deck had also been torn apart in one place'. Other damage had been inflicted 'in the after part of the ship', Langsdorff reported next day.

The fighting abilities of the ship were not seriously impaired, though ammunition for the main guns had been reduced to 40 per cent of the original stock. With the exception of the gun Dove had seen destroyed the secondary armament was intact but its ammunition supply system had been damaged. Nevertheless there remained over half its ammunition. The anti-aircraft guns had been reduced by two-thirds and its supply train destroyed; one torpedo tube was out of action but six torpedoes remained.

With the constraints on her watertight integrity, the *Admiral Graf Spee* was capable of maintaining full speed in good sea conditions. *Korvettenkapitän* Carl Klepp, the engineer commander, and his team had toiled endlessly to keep their ship's diesel engines operational during her cruise and this supererogation placed one card in Langsdorff's hand. However, the Captain concluded that: 'The ship's resources were considered inadequate for making her seaworthy . . .'

As for her people, with one officer and thirty-five ratings killed, with a further sixty men wounded, 'The reduction in fighting capacity through personnel losses was not serious'. The dead officer was *Leutnant* Grigat, who had had both legs blown off by a 6-inch shell-burst, which exploded below the foretop and also killed two seamen-rangefinders. 'He remained fully conscious until the end and must have suffered immensely . . .' Langsdorff considered his youthful 'ship's company had behaved excellently both during the action and in repairing damage after the battle'.

As the *Admiral Graf Spee* ran west, at 11.00 she encountered the *Shakespear*. Routinely ordering the British merchantman to stop, the Germans were obliged to fire a shot across her bows before she blew off steam and came to a halt. The order to abandon her was ignored, though some attempt may have been made to begin lowering the boats, an effort which was given up when it was clear that the German ship showed no sign of stopping herself. The fire-eaters aboard the *Panzerschiff* wondered why Langsdorff did not avail himself of the permission under the Prize Laws to sink her with torpedoes. It would have been an act of defiance: one in the eye for the British astern. They concluded that the damage it would do to the *Admiral Graf Spee*'s cause when she arrived in a neutral port in hope of succour put their commander off the idea. Thus it was that the German ship swept past and the *Shakespear* was left unmolested, answering Harwood's query to that effect a little later when the pursuers came up to her. Instead Langsdorff ordered a 'humanitarian' signal be made to pick up the *Shakespear*'s boats. It might delay, or slow, the pursuit a little; buy Langsdorff time to make his arrangements for entering a safe haven without interference.

Given his open style of command, Langsdorff's decision to make for the neutral port of Montevideo is odd. In making it, he took no counsel with his senior officers. This astonished – among others – his adjutant, *Leutnant* Kurt Diggins, who stated in 1959 that Langsdorff had been 'deeply impressed' by the damage to his ship, adding in this context that he had been 'wounded by shell splinters and for a short time was unconscious. It must, therefore, be assumed that he had suffered a shock which affected his subsequent decision.'

One suggestion that may have clouded Langsdorff's eagerness to effect repairs was the aggression shown by Harwood's two light cruisers in attacking with torpedoes like destroyers. They would not have done this 'if they had not been sure of support from other units in the vicinity', stated *Leutnant* Schiebusch, who had been officer-of-the-watch and close to Wattenberg throughout the action. In the light of subsequent events it is clear that Langsdorff's psychological state lent itself to the belief that overwhelming forces were not far away – a reasonable enough assumption given the time he had remained free of the effects of the Allied hue-and-cry mobilized against him.

Other, more immediate and equally fateful consequences flowed from his order to make for Montevideo, a decision that was based on both reasonable navigational arguments and ignorance. Buenos Aires would have been a more congenial destination, the government of the Argentine being pro-German, but there were certain problems in making a passage there and risking fouling the engine cooling intakes with mud if the *Admiral Graf Spee* with her deep draught, were to attempt it. Making Buenos Aires meant passing through the buoyed channel of its approaches. Montevideo was a far easier place to reach, an open roadstead off the port accessible from the ocean with less risk for a tired crew. The approach was relatively unencumbered, though a large shoal, the English Bank, lay to the southward of a vessel running westwards towards the port. Moreover, it was closer and, once within the territorial waters of a neutral nation, Harwood would be unable to renew his attack. However, Montevideo had one flaw, picked up succinctly in the German assessment: 'the great political dependence of Uruguay upon England (Britain) was not fully realized at this time by the Captain of *Spee*'.

The only other course of action was to have headed for the open ocean and attempted to affect repairs at sea, in the calmer waters of the tropics and perhaps with the resources of the *Altmark* to assist. But this was impossible, as Langsdorff well knew, whatever romantic notions his junior officers considered. The Royal Navy had a reputation for tenacity and he, in the isolation of high command, knew that with *Ajax* and *Achilles* in pursuit 'there seemed no prospect of shaking off the shadowers'. Wherever the capital ships then hunting him actually were was of little moment; it would be only a matter of time before they reached him, insufficient time in which to effect even the most basic repairs, especially to the large hole in the forepart of his ship.

For Langsdorff the decisive moment was passed when his operators transmitted battle report to the *Seekriegsleitung* to which he appended his intention to proceed to Montevideo. *Grossadmiral* Erich Raeder sent a prompt response, approving Langsdorff's plan.

And so it was for Montevideo that the *Admiral Graf Spee* made her way, thereby initiating an international diplomatic furore, committing her crew to internment, but saving 'the lives of the sons of over a thousand German mothers'.

As the pursued and her harrying pursuers approached the great estuary (the Rio de la Plata, or River Plate to the British, had been so named originally by European discoverers for the likeness of its wide waters to a sheet of silver) and the Uruguayan coast came in sight, the increasing constriction of the navigable waters brought them into contact with other ships. The wireless traffic between the *Admiral Graf Spee* and the *Ajax* regarding the *Shakespear*'s boats alerted all other merchantmen in the vicinity of the presence of this dangerous predator.

One of these was the French liner *Formose*, an early witness to the events of that evening, which were but an overture to a week-long drama that would be seen in part by thousands of Uruguayans enjoying the warm days and long, languorous evenings of the high southern summer. Aboard the *Formose*, just then passing the seaside resort of Punta del Este situated on a low, sandy peninsula 70 miles east of Montevideo, many passengers were lining the rail to stare at the sunlit buildings and beaches sliding past their starboard side a few miles away. The liner was taking the passage along the main littoral, inshore of Lobos Island, which lay some miles south-east of Punta del Este. Then a smudge of smoke appeared on their port quarter and the grey hull took shape beneath it, running fast on a course parallel but offshore of the liner's. Not far away beyond the island was the Uruguayan cruiser, the *Uruguay*, heading south-east.

Most of the *Formose*'s passengers had taken little notice of the grey ship overtaking them from seaward. They were anticipating disembarking after their long voyage from France and one ship looked much like another. Then, quite suddenly, the grey ship swung round and was enveloped in flame and smoke; the shock of the multiple concussions swept over the watchers aboard the *Formose* a few seconds later. It was obviously gunfire, but was it the *Formose* upon which those approaching guns were trained? There was no fall of shot, no plunging shells throwing up columns of white and green marbled water close to the French liner. Then the acutely sighted spotted on the eastern horizon, far astern of the grey ship, two more smudges of smoke.

On the *Formose*'s bridge the apparently senseless message about English lifeboats was suddenly comprehensible. *Capitaine* Buron, the *Formose*'s master, had had his suspicions earlier when his radio officer had handed him the intercepted signals. Mindful of his passengers and the hostile nature of the transmitting ship, he had prudently altered course to run into territorial waters as quickly as possible. Now what he had guessed was made plain fact: there was a battle in the offing and it was coming their way. As the grey ship resumed her course and came on, Buron noted the time in his logbook. It was 18.15 by the local Uruguayan zone.

*Capitán de Navio* F.J. Fuentes also observed the exchange of fire from the bridge of the *Uruguay*. The approaching *Admiral Graf Spee*, as yet unidentified, 'fired two shots in the direction of a thick mass of smoke [. . .] on the horizon'. He too noted the time.

**The Battle of the River Plate: Evening Action**
**13 December, 19.15–Midnight: 'Gloriously Silhouetted Against**
**the Afterglow'**

Between Punta del Este and Montevideo the Uruguayan coast falls back in a wide, shallow bight, open to the south and covering the 70 miles between Punta del Este, its adjacent town of Maldonado, and the city of Montevideo. The latter city culminates in a southern headland known as Punta Brava, 20 miles east of which is the small island of Flores, surmounted by a lighthouse. Twenty miles south of Flores lies the sprawl of the Banco Inglés, the English Bank, its northern extremity marked by *Pontón Faro* – a lightvessel. It was into these waters that the *Admiral Graf Spee* now led Harwood's two light cruisers.

It was now 19.00 aboard both the British and the German warships, both of which were keeping the same time. This was, however, one hour ahead of local time in Uruguay, hence the differences noted by Buron and Fuentes.

The long afternoon had passed almost without incident but at 19.15, when she had closed the distance to 12.8 miles, *Ajax* received a reminder of her adversary's ire. Langsdorff fired two salvos, the first fell short, the second plunged into the cruiser's wake as she turned away, heeling under full helm and making smoke. These were the salvos seen from the *Formose* and *Uruguay*. They were not returned, for beyond the fleeing *Panzerschiff* the friendly, Anglophile towns of Punta del Este and Maldonado lay on the line of fire. *Achilles* turned briefly, but was soon heading for Lobos Island where, in a pathetic show of fear, thousands of seals basking upon the cliffs, hurled themselves onto the rocks below at the thunder of the guns.

Harwood remained in hot pursuit as Langsdorff continued to the west, steering south of Lobos Island. Harwood signalled to Captain Parry that he was to take *Achilles* directly after Langsdorff beyond Lobos Island if – as now seemed beyond doubt – the German continued heading for Montevideo. He also 'directed *Achilles* to take every advantage of territorial waters [as cover] while shadowing'. Harwood himself, instructed Woodhouse to alter *Ajax*'s course to south-west, to pass south of Lobos Island and make for the southern extremity of the English Bank, fearful that Langsdorff would double-back round the shoal and break out to the southward – even perhaps to make for Bahía Blanca.

The courses of the two British cruisers now diverged, *Ajax* gradually peeling-off to the south-west while Parry, following Harwood's orders to the letter, steamed *Achilles* into Uruguayan waters and simultaneously reducing the distance to his quarry by passing between Lobos Island and Punta del Este. At 20.00 Harwood ordered Woodhouse to reduce speed and the *Ajax* slowed 'to watch events'. Ten minutes later and about forty minutes behind the *Panzerschiff*, the *Achilles* swept past Punta del Este. At 20.48 the *Admiral Graf Spee* reached the Uruguayan 3-mile limit and Langsdorff turned her directly into the glare of a 'magnificent sunset [. . .] and she chose this moment, while the sunlight was in the eyes of the British gunlayers, to turn sufficiently to make both turrets bear'. Then she fired three salvos at the *Achilles*. Parry put his helm over as the first two landed short and had the satisfaction of the third bursting in his wake. With a starboard turn *Achilles* now entered Uruguayan waters and was less than 3 miles offshore, a fact being industriously plotted by Fuentes and his officers aboard the *Uruguay*, which, as the two belligerent ships passed to the north, had swung round and was following the dramatic action.

There were some complexities attached to the territoriality or otherwise of these waters. On establishing her own independence from Spain shortly after the end of the Napoleonic Wars, Argentina had possessed both banks of the Rio de la Plata, but in 1828 she had agreed to the secession and independent status of the Oriental Province of Uruguay. She had not, however, conceded a claim to a 9-mile coastal strip of territorial waters advanced by the new country; neither had Great Britain. An accommodation had been reached between the two countries that established to their mutual satisfaction that the estuary was not open water, but 'enclosed' west of a line between Punta del Este and Cape San Antonio over 100 miles away on the Argentinian coast. By now the opposing forces were within this area, which in theory was divided between Argentina and Uruguay, but which in reality remained 'disputed' by the two states. British Admiralty rules of engagement in 1939 insisted only upon respect being accorded to a 3-mile limit. A warship might pass through territorial waters up to 3 miles off a littoral state, but were not supposed to engage in belligerent action. However, the legality of the situation was affected by the case of 'hot pursuit' and while it might be argued that the British were harrying the German *Panzerschiff*, they were – under international law – entitled to respond to an attack in self-defence.

Mindful of these considerations Parry, having just pulled *Achilles* clear to the south of the 3-mile limit in passing Punta Negra, nevertheless opened fire. The *Admiral Graf Spee* was now 'gloriously silhouetted against the afterglow [of sunset]' wrote Washbourn still in *Achilles*'s fire direction tower, 'and we must have been nearly invisible . . .' This was an ironic reversal of Craddock's fate at the hands of Reichsgraf von Spee in 1914. To counter this Langsdorff ordered a smokescreen laid in her wake. With *Achilles* following 'just outside the 3-mile limit, that we admit, but inside the [9-mile] territorial waters claimed'. Langsdorff's fire provided Parry and his gunnery officer Washbourn with 'the excuse, and with delight I again muttered SHOOT into my transmitter'. Washbourn went on:

> There was only time for five very nice broadsides before things became too hot for us, and we turned away again under smoke. Marvellous shooting on her part, considering the poor target that we presented [. . .] we did achieve a straddle or two according to our flank mark *Ajax*.

It was now 20.54 and the two ships continued running west at full speed with the lights of Montevideo looming 20 miles ahead. To keep her persistent tormentor at bay as the swifter *Achilles* closed the distance at a speed of 30 knots, Langsdorff ordered Ascher to throw salvos into the threatening darkness astern at 21.32, 21.40 and 21.43.

Parry did not respond to these as the two ships were rapidly closing the island of Flores, moreover the fall of shot persuaded him that the German gunlayers had no exact idea of *Achilles*'s position and were firing deterrent shots. Seventeen minutes later, with Flores almost abeam to starboard and distant 3 miles, *Achilles* was only 5 miles from the *Admiral Graf Spee*. As the last glimmers of twilight faded, the growing lights of the city of refuge ahead of her threw the *Panzerschiff*'s silhouette into sharp relief to the watching Parry and Washbourn. With her considerable advantage in speed and proximity to the *Admiral Graf Spee*, there might yet be a chance to launch a torpedo attack. But such a worthy and appropriate *coup de grâce* was denied Parry, for Harwood, lying beyond the Banco Inglés, aware that *Achilles* was a mere 11 miles from Montevideo, called off the chase.

It was 22.17 and Parry ordered *Achilles* to reduce speed and put her helm over. Shortly afterwards she passed the watching *Uruguay* and the inward-bound *Formose*, rejoining Harwood offshore. The two actions known as the Battle of the River Plate were over, but the drama was not yet concluded and the British Commodore settled down to blockade his enemy and await events. The *Achilles* patrolled the waters between Flores and the lightvessel off the English Bank; the *Ajax* blocked the escape route south of the shoal. In the meantime Harwood prepared and transmitted his report of the action to the Admiralty in London. It had been a long day.

As the *Admiral Graf Spee* approached Montevideo and slowed her speed to 18 knots, Langsdorff announced to her crew over the public-address system that: 'From today there is no more war for us!' It was a fateful moment, though few among his listeners could have realized it in all its implications. Assisted by one of his mercantile reserve officers who was familiar with the port, Langsdorff brought the *Admiral Graf Spee* into the outer, or ante, port and, at about 23.30 by her own time, the *Panzerschiff* let go her anchor and brought up off Montevideo. Then her main engines fell silent.

In the appropriated midshipmen's quarters the British captives woke from their uneasy dozing. Such a sudden change in the normal noise of bustle acted upon all their seamanlike instincts. The quiet was eventually broken by the rasp of locks and then *Oberleutnant* Herzberg and the guards were in the doorway. Dove approached him, asking what had happened. Herzberg placed his hand upon the British master's shoulder and raised his voice to address them all.

# Evening Action: 13 December, 19.15–Midnight

'Gentlemen, for you the war is over. We are now anchored in Montevideo harbour and the Captain has told me to say that you will be free tomorrow.'

For a moment disbelief struck them all and then several moved to stare through the damage and caught sight of the blazing lights of a neutral port, a port in which it was impossible under International Law for them to continue to be held as prisoners of war. 'The hoot of taxis and the whistle of trains came faintly [. . .] over the water . . .'

Then the relief led to cheering and finally a euphoria that prevented sleep from coming until near dawn.

## Three Days of Uncertainty
### 14–16 December: 'This Is Not a Friendly Port to Germany'

The lighthouse keeper at Punta del Este had been the first to alert the outside world that a naval action was taking place off the Rio de la Plata. He telephoned the editor of a Montevideo newspaper, who treated the intermittent information as a sequence of news bulletins. But it was an American reporter, Mike Fowler, who became central to the broadcasting of the sequence of events that, in the coming week, transfixed global interest.

British merchant ships in Montevideo were made aware that something was up about noon on the 13th when 'a report came in that the *Achilles* had been sunk', whereupon 'the local Nazis began to celebrate, but their jubilation was shortlived. Towards 7 p.m.,' wrote the Houlder Line shipping agent to his sister, 'reports came along from the lighthouse keeper [. . .] that a large unknown warship was coming along at full speed followed by the *Exeter*, *Ajax* and *Achilles*.' Crowds began to assemble as the fighting could be seen from the shore; then news arrived that 'the *Exeter* had fallen out of the chase'. The German ship 'had quite a lot of damage [. . .] repairs [commenced] immediately', and went on 'feverishly all day on the 14th, 15th and 16th up to 2 a.m. on the 17th. All the time the damaged little British cruisers kept the seas, buried their dead, and tended their wounded as best they could. But they never left their watch on the port.' Captain Daniel, the writer of this letter, was not only a master-mariner; he had held a commission in the Royal Naval

Reserve and was understandably moved by the pluck of the 'little British cruisers' and their dogged keeping of the sea.

Behind Daniel's synopsis of events lay a fervid activity, not just on the part of the *Admiral Graf Spee*'s crew. As the German warship had approached Montevideo the commander of the Uruguayan corvette *Huracan* offered medical assistance to both sides. Harwood politely declined and while Langsdorff did not accept, his plight was obvious to *Capitán de Fragata* José Varela and an engineering lieutenant who went aboard immediately the *Panzerschiff* entered Montevideo. They were astonished at 'a certain confusion among the young crew', the wreckage lying on the upper deck and the dead and wounded. Again Langsdorff was asked if help could be rendered and, while he retained most of his wounded in the care of his own medical staff, he requested one man, 'a gunner rating who had been wounded in the eyes and face' be removed to a hospital. Five more followed later, at 01.30, when Langsdorff had had his surgeon's reports and better assessed the situation.

Varela asked Langsdorff why he had entered the port at night without navigation lights, to which he received the reply that the British cruisers had violated International Law by firing on the *Admiral Graf Spee* when within the 3-mile limit. The claim was the opening salvo of another battle, of diplomacy, negotiation and deception. Langsdorff, on the evidence of Rasenack, first requested a long stay of fifteen days, during which repairs could be effected and German U-boats could race to their assistance and nullify the effects of a British surface blockade outside the port. The neutral Uruguayans offered forty-eight hours, the time allowed British warships to come into the port to reprovision. Langsdorff's request did not receive the support of the German minister in Montevideo. Herr Otto Langmann thought it a matter of honour that a German warship should require no longer a period in port than a British, despite the difference in their circumstances. Langmann and Langsdorff fell out over this, though they preserved a united front in public.

In addition to this first diplomatic rebuff, Langsdorff was subject to further pressures. While *Ajax* and *Achilles* could be seen from the damaged gunnery control position, other forces were *thought* to be arriving. Reports that 'our worst enemy' the battlecruiser HMS *Renown*, could be seen from the gunnery control position began to circulate. Entirely imagined as this in fact was, it played powerfully into the hands of the British and worked a corrosive effect upon every member of the *Admiral Graf Spee*'s crew. Even *within* the port the German sailors were reminded of Great Britain's sea power, fulminated Rasenack, so it was not difficult to extrapolate a little imaginatively on circumstances outside:

> It seems an irony of fate that days on end we cruised around the sea routes without seeing as much as the top of a mast of a British merchantman on the horizon and now they are all around us, flying the British flag. Each ship is armed with a gun on the stern.

With a stay in port of forty-eight hours, the *Admiral Graf Spee*'s demoralized crew was galvanized into action. The positive directions stiffened their resolve and they received technical help and equipment from two German merchant ships in the port, one of which was the *Tacoma*, but not from any local companies of note. Nevertheless, some help was forthcoming. In addition to the assistance rendered by the German merchantmen, a contractor of sorts was found in the German-owned Ribereña Del Plata Coal Company, and ex-patriate German workers employed in Montevideo came forward. Increasing help came from Buenos Aires, not least from the representatives of German firms who helped with some of the specialized repairs. Notable among these were the elevator engineers, Cippola and Siemens, who worked on the damaged ammunition hoists. Meanwhile the lookout in the foretop kept a sharp eye on the seaward horizon. During that first day, the 14th, news of the arrival of a battleship spread 'like fire' through the ship.

Langsdorff was himself convinced of the presence of Allied warships offshore. In his farewell to Captain Dove he admired the gallantry of the *Exeter*'s crew, who did not know when they were beaten, and the pugnacity of the light cruisers who 'came at me like destroyers'. He admitted to Dove that: 'I said to myself, "They would

*Tacoma*

never do this unless they were supported by big ships.'' Now, he told Dove, the British battleship *Barham* and the French *Dunkerque* lay in waiting for him. 'This is not a friendly port to Germany,' Langsdorff concluded.

Later that day Dove and the other merchant officers mustered on the quarter-deck beside the *Swastika*-draped coffins of the *Admiral Graf Spee*'s thirty-six dead. Then they were dismissed and left the ship, free men.

The failure of local firms, especially the Montevideo Dock Company, to assist with repairs incensed the Germans. 'They belong to British capital,' Rasenack complained, enumerating the impossibility of the tasks confronting them. In fact this seems inaccurate, for the 'only ship repair yard in Montevideo' was Uruguayan-owned, though the managing director, Señor Voulminot, had a French father. When confronted, Voulminot said that that was only one reason. Overriding this was the fact that he was a Uruguayan. According to Millington-Drake, Hitler's policies and methods were inimical to the Uruguayan ideal of democracy.

Ignoring Langmann, Langsdorff claimed the right of sufficient time to render his ship seaworthy, basing this on the large and obvious shell-hole in the *Admiral Graf Spee*'s bow. His opponent in this diplomatic wrangle was Eugen Millington-Drake, the very sociable, eccentric and popular British minister who, mindful of the dangers in delay largely residing in the arrival of U-boats, supported the stand of the Uruguayan ministry against a long stay. Under Articles 12, 14 and

## Three Days of Uncertainty: 14–16 December

17 of the Hague Convention Millington-Drake argued the *Admiral Graf Spee* should be allowed no more than twenty-four hours' respite, on the basis that because she had steamed 300 miles at full speed since the action, she was not unseaworthy. If she stayed longer, Millington-Drake said, she should be interned. He was joined by the French Minister, M. Gentil, who stressed the points already made. Millington-Drake had enjoyed a long-standing friendship with Dr Guani, the Uruguayan minister across whose desk this battle increased in intensity. Both the Allied diplomats pressed Guani, holding over him the spectre of the threat implicit in the guns of the *Admiral Graf Spee* being pointed at his city.

As the day drew to its close Langsdorff summoned all his officers into their mess and explained the position. He displayed 'his well-known optimism', stating that he did not wish the ship to be interned; submission to this would mean the Uruguayans would confiscate the ship and she would be acquired by the British. This was unthinkable. Instead they would break out at night, using the cover of mist. Langsdorff's disenchantment with the help, or lack of it, offered by Langmann, threw him back on his own resources; it was regrettable that they had not made directly for Buenos Aires; now, unfortunately, they could not cross the estuary directly, owing to navigational constraints. Avoiding re-engagement with Harwood's waiting cruisers was unavoidable. However, having the *Admiral Graf Spee* interned in Argentina was preferable: they could present her to the Argentine Navy in the same way that SMSs *Goeben* and *Breslau* had been 'given' to Turkey after their defiant run through the Mediterranean in the First World War.

Asked for their opinion, the officers did not match Langsdorff's mood. There were eight British merchantmen within the port and they would broadcast a warning if the German ship moved, undeterred by the £5 fine any such infringement of port regulations would attract. Moreover, the staff of the British legation would have the ship under surveillance. Langsdorff withdrew to draft his report of the action.

At the same time, out at sea, Commodore Harwood had just received the reinforcement of HMS *Cumberland*. He had ideas quite contrary to Millington-Drake and wished the sailing of the *Admiral Graf Spee* to be delayed as long as possible. Accordingly he had earlier that day signalled the British embassy at Buenos Aires, where the nearest British embassy was located – only a legation being maintained at Montevideo – that he wished Millington-Drake to arrange for the eight British merchantmen in harbour to depart from that port at twenty-four hour intervals. Under International Law a belligerent warship could not be sailed within twenty-four hours of the departure of a merchantman, in order to give the civilian vessel a fair chance of escape. This delay would enable further British reinforcements to arrive, removing all possibility of any advantage accruing to Langsdorff's ship if he emerged to fight. In short, Harwood would add substance to the spectral Allied men-of-war already in the collective minds' eyes of the Germans, but he needed five days to accomplish this. Given that time, *Renown* would indeed be on-scene, along with the carrier *Ark Royal*, the cruisers *Neptune*, *Dorsetshire* and *Shropshire*, and three destroyers.

Harwood's request did not reach Millington-Drake until next morning, but by then, with the additional support of Fallowfield's *Cumberland*, Harwood had blocked all channels and arranged for the three cruisers to withdraw to a rendezvous offshore from which concentration-point they would attack the emerging *Admiral Graf Spee*. The British naval attaché in Buenos Aires, Captain H. McCall, now joined ex-Army captain Rex Miller, the MI6 agent in Montevideo, whose office window commanded the harbour. McCall arrived from Buenos Aires to join Miller in a circuit of the *Admiral Graf Spee* to assess the damage she had sustained and report to Millington-Drake. British diplomatic pressure now matched her sea power against the beleaguered Germans.

Although all this 'necessitated a disconcerting change of diplomatic tactics' for Millington-Drake, he rose to the occasion and arranged with her master that the SS *Ashworth* should sail at 18.15 on Saturday evening, 16 December. This would confine the *Panzerschiff* until the same time Sunday evening. A note to Guani, invoking the appropriate clauses of the Hague Convention, also prompted surprise at the British change of tack. Guani strove to be even-handed, contacting the Foreign Minister of Panama, from whence had come the Pan-American declaration of a neutral zone in October, but in the event he was able only to function as an umpire in the battle of diplomacy and deception that now raged over the Rio de la Plata.

In the small hours of Friday, 15 December Langsdorff's *Report of Proceedings* was transmitted to Berlin. That morning a small detachment of officers and ratings – all that could be spared from the urgent repair-work – accompanied the thirty-six coffins in a tug. The British masters who had been released had been asked to stay away but a number of them, led by Dove, made an appearance at the German cemetery and laid a wreath in tribute 'To the Memory of brave men of the sea from their comrades of the British Merchant Service'. This 'chivalrous act' filled Rasenack and his shipmates 'with grateful appreciation'. In the meanwhile the German crew performed prodigies of ingenuity and sheer hard work, being visited by a Uruguayan commission who examined the *Admiral Graf Spee*'s condition. They granted an extension of the *Admiral Graf Spee*'s stay in port to seventy-two hours and placed a guard over her, the corvette *Lavelleja*. This had been in response to the insistence of Millington-Drake who, with Captain McCall, had waited upon Dr Guani late that night. Offshore, the reports from the foretop that day had insisted the blockaders had been reinforced by an aircraft carrier. The Uruguayan radio reports seemed to confirm these sightings.

The rumours, specious sightings and general mood on board the *Admiral Graf Spee* were fertile soil for the planting of conspiracy theories in the coming few days. The mysterious darkened ship that had passed them shortly before the action and which Langsdorff had declined to attack was blamed for betraying their position and providing the British with warning of their descent upon the Rio de la Plata. 'News' that the British were chasing the *Altmark* was linked with the departure of the British masters, not all of whom had been so friendly or sympathetic as Dove. 'Some [had] said goodbye ironically . . .' remembered Rasenack, '. . . others pityingly.'

Such speculations were to be expected on the ship; ashore Langsdorff continued to wrestle with the authorities, advising Berlin of the further development of the arrival of *Renown* and *Ark Royal*.

# The Battle of the River Plate

All chances of escape to the open sea 'and getting through to Germany' were gone. He could, he thought, 'fight my way through to Buenos Aires' but since this might result in the loss of the ship 'without the possibility of causing damage to the enemy, [I] request instructions whether to scuttle the ship (in spite of the inadequate depth of water in the Plate estuary) or submit to internment'. Langmann added his own comments, asking for 'an urgent decision regarding Spee'. He added: 'Superior enemy forces which have been clearly established from on board Spee make it appear to the Commanding Officer quite out of the question to [. . .] achieve a successful break through to Germany.' Langmann concluded that he agreed with his naval attaché, Kapitän zur See Dietrich Niebuhr, that internment would be 'the worst possible solution' and that 'in view of her shortage of ammunition' it would be best 'to blow her up [. . .] and have the crew interned'.

Langsdorff made no mention of the condition of his ship's engines, or of damage to the lens in the foretop rangefinder, both entered in the ship's *War Diary*. The German Foreign Ministry instructed Langsdorff and Langmann to seek the longest possible visit and 'counter [. . .] the influence of the British'.

That evening Langsdorff spoke 'with some of the crew who [. . .] [were] standing near him' telling them that if he could not break the blockade he would scuttle the ship. 'This news spreads rapidly through the ship.' As an experienced commander Langsdorff knew that on board ship a hard fact is better than the corrosion of rumour.

The British cruisers offshore found Friday 15th and Saturday 16th, 'particularly trying', being relatively close inshore and closed-up on watch-and-watch. Lewin and Kearney flew off on a dawn patrol in the Fairey Seafox 'before the quite excellent reporting system off Montevideo had become established'. Lewin 'was so tired by this time, that I was constantly falling asleep in the air, which was not good for either Kearney's or my nervous systems.'

By Sunday 'the quite excellent reporting system' was up and running. The plight of the German warship had so caught the world's imagination at this early and – for many – exciting stage of the war that a dockside running commentary was set up by Mike Fowler. It was conveniently in English.

# Three Days of Uncertainty: 14–16 December

Apart from the *Cumberland*, filling the gap left by the *Exeter*, Harwood had as yet received none of the reinforcements attributed to him by his enemies. He had had support of another kind, fuel by favour of the Royal Fleet Auxiliary tanker *Olythus*, Captain L.N. Hill, which was pumped into *Ajax* on Friday in a rough sea. *Achilles* was topped up in like manner on Sunday.

Next morning, Saturday, 16 December, was a wet day. Rain did not prevent weekend crowds coming down to the waterfront to observe what could be seen of the international drama on their doorstep, a drama now being broadcast to the world by Mike Fowler. Intended for an American audience, Fowler's relentless verbal descriptions reached the mess decks of the three British cruisers within seven seconds. This had been largely facilitated by the initiative of the Marconi representative in Montevideo, John Garland, who with Millington-Drake – the latter having provided cash for the equipment from his own pocket – set up a receiving station for signals from ships at sea. These could then be retransmitted via the local radio station to the Falklands and London. This was set up in the British consulate and was manned by ex-patriate friends of Garland. To increase the roster, upon their discharge from the *Admiral Graf Spee*, a number of the radio officers from sunken British merchantmen were recruited. All were on contract to Marconi, who in turn hired them to shipping companies. This was all backed up by mobilizing the radio room of another British merchant ship in port, the Houlder liner *Linton Grange* – though in theory her wireless was 'sealed' when in port. This unofficial link, with whom the Uruguayan post office telegraphists co-operated, was estimated to cut over five hours over the standard transmission times for messages from Montevideo to London.

On board the *Admiral Graf Spee*, still lying at anchor, Langsdorff cleared the lower deck and addressed his crew. He appeared to have recovered his spirits and they understood that Berlin had instructed Langsdorff not to allow the Uruguayans to intern their ship. Having raised morale, Langsdorff was obliged to sustain it. Perhaps it was this demand upon the professional soul of the man that gave him his appearance of outward calm and confident resolution; perhaps too he had made his own pact with destiny. Something seemed to be afoot, for the crew observed that the *Tacoma* had moved, to place her bulk between the *Admiral Graf Spee* and the shore, frustrating the observers, casual or otherwise.

In contrast to Fowler's broadcasts, the low rain and overcast cloud helped the Germans a little. Lewin and Kearney, carrying out an early forenoon reconnaissance flight in the *Ajax*'s Seafox, reported nothing visible. Meanwhile Harwood had received revised rules of engagement from the Admiralty: he could fight anywhere outside the 3-mile limit. Mindful that any close action off the port might result in shells landing ashore, he withdrew the ships a little. Signalling the details to his squadron he began: 'My object destruction . . .'

In pursuance of his own instructions Millington-Drake had arranged for the second British merchant ship to sail at 17.00 that evening (6 p.m. Montevideo time). This would be the Houlder Brothers' refrigerated cargo liner *Dunster Grange*. Other machinations were in progress. Knowing the telephone lines between the British legation in Montevideo and the embassy in Buenos Aires were tapped, McCall put in a call to the ambassador, Sir Edmund Ovey, telling Ovey that he had an important message. When Ovey protested the phone line was too exposed, McCall cunningly riposted that the message was of the utmost urgency and could not wait; the risk of eavesdropping had to be accepted. McCall then asked for 2,000 tons of boiler oil to be available for two British capital ships at the Argentine naval base at Mar del Plata. Realizing the ruse, Ovey then set the request in train, along with enquiries about the adequacy of port facilities to cope with *Renown* and *Ark Royal*. Elsewhere disinformation of the imminent arrival of these two heavy warships was disseminated, a propaganda coup that was entirely successful to the extent of their ghostly presence being 'seen' off Punta del Este.

Throughout the day the diplomatic shuffle went on. The Uruguayan minister stood firm on the duration of the *Admiral Graf Spee*'s stay, but suspended all sailings of merchantmen as from that evening, after the departure of the *Dunster Grange*. In distant Berlin a series of high-ranking conferences took place. The first was led by *Grossadmiral* Erich Raeder, Commander-in-Chief of the *Kriegsmarine*.

# Three Days of Uncertainty: 14–16 December

Raeder's summary of the overwhelming forces confronting Langsdorff was challenged by *Fregattenkapitän* Wagner, who protested the impossibility of *Ark Royal* and *Renown* having joined Harwood. Admiral Schniewind, the Chief of Staff, argued Langsdorff as the man-on-the-spot 'must have made certain of his facts'. Raeder agreed; deferring to the commander on-scene was both common sense and a mark of confidence. Langsdorff must be left a free hand. Having cleared the matter in a further meeting with Hitler, the core of the instructions transmitted to the *Admiral Graf Spee* were that a breakout to Buenos Aires was authorized but, if that proved impossible, internment was not to be considered. The only permitted alternative – destruction – was to be effective and thorough.

Late that afternoon Langsdorff summoned Kay, his equal in rank but junior in seniority, and Wattenberg. The three officers were joined by Niebuhr. Langsdorff reiterated what they all knew: no extension of their stay would be countenanced; that even if they succeeded in breaking through the British – which Harwood himself was even then estimating at about a 70 per cent chance – the condition of the *Panzerschiff* was not such that she could reach Germany. If they did engage the enemy in shallow waters on the chance of inflicting damage to her tormentors, the navigational constraints limited manoeuvre and the shallow water meant that the ship might ground and be humiliatingly shot to pieces. It was thought, somewhat fancifully, that if she remained in defiance of the Uruguayan government's orders, the British ships might close in and sink her in the port. A breakthrough to Buenos Aires was unlikely to succeed owing to the mud in the river; reduction in the intake of cooling water would be catastrophic to the ailing engines and, again, they risked being shot to pieces by the shallower-draughted British cruisers. This was an ironic consequence of the German bending of the limitations of the Washington Treaty.

Langsdorff finally gave orders for a scuttling outside territorial waters. All subsequent wrangling, inter-ministerial contact, exchange of diplomatic notes, protests or opinion from a distant *Seekriegsleitung* was of little consequence. The *Admiral Graf Spee*'s fate was decided upon.

# The Battle of the River Plate

The German warship had been under constant scrutiny from the morning after her arrival. This had been organized by Houlder's agent, Captain Daniel, who had gathered a coterie of British pensioners 'who had been soldiers in the last war, and stationed them in British ships in the bay, maintaining a constant watch day and night'. A good vantage point had been found aboard a tramp belonging to the Hain Steamship Co of St Ives, 'which was berthed between the *Graf Spee* and the *Tacoma*'.

Loads of lifebelts 'and other gear' had been reported moved from the *Tacoma* and it was becoming clear to Daniel that it could be expected that the *Admiral Graf Spee* would probably move overnight on Saturday/Sunday. It was also observed that between about 15.00 and 19.30 'the crew were mustered repeatedly on the *Graf Spee*'s after-deck, and addressed by one officer after another. The last officer to address them was the Captain himself [. . .] but the repair work went on feverishly'.

The British observers saw that work on deck stopped at 02.00. Below decks, however, the emphasis had shifted from repair to 'effective' destruction. As twilight gave way to dawn over the sleeping city individual officers gave detailed instructions to their working parties and sections. Cartridge ammunition was to be detonated deep in the ship to destroy the central fire-control system; the breech-blocks of the guns were removed. At noon Langsdorff held another meeting, informing the officers that tugs and barges would arrive from Buenos Aires to embark and withdraw all but the skeleton crew, who would attend the ship to her grave.

That afternoon Commodore Harwood was handed a signal. With effect from 13 December he had been promoted rear admiral; he had, moreover, been made a Knight Commander of the Bath. Bell, Parry and Woodhouse had been made Commanders of the Bath. A wit on board *Ajax* was heard to point out the lack of logic of the British establishment: as a result of battle damage, neither Harwood nor Woodhouse possessed a bathroom between them. Communicating the news to the squadron, Harwood thanked all hands for their actions in the battle.

# Sunset 17 December: 'That Was That'

**Sunset**

**17 December: 'That Was That'**

Sunday, 17 December 1939 found the *Admiral Graf Spee* still in Montevideo. Popular opinion had thought she would make a run under cover of darkness and now the clock was ticking. As Fowler told America and the world, she would have to have sailed by eight o'clock that evening, local time, or submit to internment. He asked the rhetorical question as to whether Langsdorff would sail and risk action with the 'five, possibly seven' British warships waiting for him? Would he 'fight to the death' or 'make a dash for Buenos Aires'? The tension increased in all quarters throughout the day. On board the *Panzerschiff* the preparations for scuttling went on. Ascher, among others, insisted on separate demolition circuits, which precluded Langsdorff himself firing the charges. Instead, his officers insisted, the Captain should be available to look after the crew and should therefore take no risks. There is a hint in Rasenack's account that Langsdorff had intended to destroy his own life simultaneously with that of his ship. The robust build of the *Admiral Graf Spee* presented the officers with certain problems, but the demolition centred on the five remaining torpedo heads being placed under the main turrets and the engine room. These were fused with grenades connected to batteries. The circuits were to be closed by the hands of five synchronized chronometers. Above the torpedo heads in the base of the turrets were stacked shells and bags of black gunpowder. Into these explosives went a few other pieces of equipment for destruction, the gun breeches included. Rasenack for one buried his ceremonial sword under the forward turret, retaining only his short dirk to surrender to the Argentine authorities in due course.

Meanwhile, as they finished their tasks, the ship's company of the *Admiral Graf Spee* were being transferred by launch to the *Tacoma*. Fowler observed them carrying their kit and being smartly spirited below decks. All but forty-three officers and ratings had been mustered in the alleyways below decks at noon, ready to leave their ship. When they arrived aboard the *Tacoma* they were to go below and not to show themselves on deck.

# The Battle of the River Plate

That afternoon Dr Guani summoned all the diplomatic representatives, the heads of missions and ambassadors, of all the American nations in Montevideo to explain both his actions and the pressures he had been put under by the representatives of the belligerent powers. These did not end, for an hour later Millington-Drake, aware of the transfer of 'over 700 men' to the *Tacoma*, insisted that Guani intern her. It was now clear that Langsdorff had narrowed his options to two: scuttling or a dash to Buenos Aires with a skeleton crew.

By the late afternoon crowds of sightseers – curiosity augmenting the Sunday-evening *paseo* – had gathered all along the waterfront of Montevideo and beyond. Langsdorff had, meanwhile, notified the harbour authorities that the *Admiral Graf Spee* would sail about 18.15, local time. The news was quickly common knowledge.

The senior officers left last. Kay, the ship's executive officer in charge of the bulk of the crew, ordered Wattenberg the navigator 'to look after our Captain', an injunction, Wattenberg wrote afterwards, 'which showed his preoccupation that he would try to seek death with his ship'.

At 18.30, as the sun began its descent in a clear sky and at the close of a beautiful day, the capstans on the *Panzerschiff*'s foredeck began to weigh her anchor. Watching from a porthole aboard the *Tacoma*, Rasenack wrote afterwards of 'a deplorable ending' as the *Admiral Graf Spee* swung to head for the harbour entrance and gathered headway, the ship's wind lifting the great *Swastika*-emblazoned battle ensign. 'The moment,' he concluded, 'was a bitter one.'

For those left on board, each stood at their post 'alone with his thoughts'. Langsdorff said little beyond the necessary conning orders as the ship steamed south, clear of the territorial waters of Uruguay.

The *Admiral Graf Spee* was followed by her own launches and then the *Tacoma*, whose departure was illegal and challenged by the *Lavelleja*, which tracked the two German ships and their launches, and was followed by several Uruguayan tugs commandeered by the harbour authorities.

Along the shoreline 'thousands and thousands of people were waving goodbye and some [were] weeping at the dockside'. Fowler's

# Sunset 17 December: 'That Was That'

broadcasts had enticed, according to Captain Daniel, 'about two hundred thousand people'. They had come to see the *Admiral Graf Spee* fight and there was no cheering, 'for the Germans are not popular here'. The turn to the westwards, into the stream to anchor and not to seaward, came as a surprise to the watching crowds who 'were amazed . . .'

Offshore the three British cruisers moved west towards sunset, knowing the German ship had to leave harbour. It was, Washbourn recalled: 'A glorious, clear evening with a vivid sunset over the Argentine coast [. . .] We were closed up and loaded, ready for whatever might come . . .'

Aboard *Ajax*, Rear Admiral Sir Henry Harwood ordered Woodhouse to launch the Fairey Seafox. Once again Lewin and Kearney climbed into their aeroplane and gave the thumbs-up to the catapult's crew.

As the *Admiral Graf Spee* closed the intended position of scuttling, 3 miles clear of the shore, two tugs and a lighter were not far away, having been sent from Buenos Aires. The way was run off the *Panzerschiff* and the anchor let go. The charges were set to detonate after a delay of twenty minutes, during which the skeleton crew dropped into a launch for transfer to the *Tacoma*. 'At the very last,' Wattenberg wrote, 'we five officers gathered with our Captain on the quarterdeck, the flag and pennant were hauled down and then we got into the Captain's launch which had also come alongside. We went about a mile away and then awaited the moment until the fuse should do its work . . .'

At the moment of detonation a column of flame rose from the ship and the *Admiral Graf Spee* looked like 'a volcano'. Rasenack saw:

Ever more columns of fire leap forth [. . .] I can see clearly how two of the big guns of the stern turret are turned in the air as if they were toothpicks. The cloud of the main explosion rises to over 300 metres and still the explosions go on. The *Graf Spee* is enveloped in flames.

Another of the detonation party, the chief mechanic Hans Götz, thought the stern 'had broken off. A sea of fire stretched from stem to stern'. Langsdorff ordered Wattenberg, who had the ship's logbook in his charge, to note the time as 20.00 and the fact that the *Admiral Graf Spee* had been put out of commission.

From the shore the initial departure of the *Admiral Graf Spee* had been obscured by a light mist in the still air, but her turn into the stream as she anchored was clearly visible against 'one of those gorgeous South American sunsets', wrote Daniel, in an epitaph that sums up the drama of the moment and is all the more poignant coming from the pen of a seaman:

> full of brilliant colours, from red-gold on the skyline, fading off into yellow, pale green and blue, and violet overhead where a lone star shone. At the right edge of the picture lay the extreme point of the coastline. To the middle left, outlined clear against the sunset, lay the merchant ship *Tacoma* and the tugs [. . .]
>
> Still farther to the left and a long way out to seaward, where the shades of evening dimmed the line between sea and sky, could be seen the flicker of a Morse lamp and the flash of a distant searchlight of an inquisitive British cruiser; and in the centre of the picture, rising high into the heavens a sombre column of dense black smoke from a vivid flame that was a funeral pyre of the dangerous German raider.

The first detonation was followed by 'more explosions and in a little while she was ablaze from end to end and all up the tower too. It was a wonderful sight against the sunset', wrote the Hon. Jean Shaw (daughter of Lord Craigmyle, then Chairman of P & O), who was then working at the British Hospital.

High above flew the *Ajax*'s Seafox. Lewin had 'a grandstand view' that was 'Wagnerian. *Graf Spee* was silhouetted against the sun, which to us had not yet set' as, in a 'fantastic series of explosions [. . .] she destroyed herself'. They transmitted the signal '*Graf Spee* has just blown herself up,' to the waiting squadron. Neither Lewin nor Kearney were impressed with the delay they experienced in being picked up. Upon receipt of their message all hands aboard the British cruisers were ordered to leave their battle stations and muster on deck, to crowd every vantage point and 'see the last of their old enemy'. Washbourn recalled that 'enormous moment':

> *Ajax,* leading us, either forgot to make a signal to tell us that she had reduced [speed] or we weren't troubling about signals at the time. We shot up on her, sheered out, and as the two ships passed close to in the gathering twilight there was the most magnificent spontaneous expression of feeling, and each ship cheered the other until no one had any voice left [. . .] I don't expect ever to feel or witness anything like that again.

The German crew were transferred from the launches and the *Tacoma* into the two Argentine tugs, the *Gigante* and the *Coloso*, and the lighter *Chirguana* outside territorial waters. Some interference was experienced from tugs from Montevideo, but the transfer was effected minus the *Panzerschiff*'s civilian Chinese laundrymen, who were taken by the Uruguayans.

The demolition party withdrawing in the launches were intercepted by the corvette *Zapican*, aboard which Langsdorff and Ascher clambered while Götz and the rest of them 'waited in the boat with our Mauser pistols at hand in our pockets'. They did not catch up with the *Gigante*, *Coloso* and the lighter until 'the middle of the night' (though Langsdorff appears to have taken part in the altercation with the Uruguayan tugs) whereupon they 'climbed on board and let the motor boat float away. So ended the cruise on which we started so hopefully and happily'.

It was now dark and as the Argentine vessels moved away without lights the burning ship 'a torch in the darkness [. . .] one of the English cruisers appears and turns her searchlights onto the remains of the *Graf Spee* . . .' A cold wind blew as the men in the lighter huddle 'like sardines in a box'. They made for Buenos Aires, crouching and waiting for the dawn.

For Wattenberg, withdrawing in defeat, 'It was a shattering sight', for Washbourn, in victory, there was the moment of anti-climax, the awful consequence summed up by Wellington on the evening of

# The Battle of the River Plate

Waterloo that the only thing worse than a battle lost, was a battle won. As the Germans escaped in the darkness aboard their hired tugs and the towed lighter, Harwood's two light cruisers moved towards the burning wreck.

> Gradually the burning hulk came up over the horizon. The Germans had made a very thorough job of it. She burnt fiercely with small explosions every few minutes [. . .] Towards midnight we approached within a few miles of the pyre, and then turned away and resumed our various patrols. That night we relaxed and [. . .] for the first time, neglected our dawn action stations. And that was that.

The *Admiral Graf Spee* settled on the bottom in latitude 34° 58' 25" South, Longitude 056° 18' 01" West and was to sink gradually into the ooze of the Rio de la Plata, finally disappearing in 1950.

# Aftermath

Writing to his wife, Harwood afterwards confessed his embarrassment that he had been: 'Showered with honours before the job was done,' betraying his anxiety as to the outcome as he waited outside Montevideo. Finally, the news from Lewin and Kearney that the *Admiral Graf Spee* had blown herself up brought him relief. Washbourn had said: 'that was that', and yet it was not over, for there was a long aftermath to this battle.

For the Germans arriving off Buenos Aires, claiming disingenuously to be shipwrecked seamen, there was a welcome of sorts. Food was available, but Ovey had pointed out to the Argentine authorities that their country's dependency upon exporting her meat and other products to Britain could be ruined by their support of German commerce raiding. In due course the *Admiral Graf Spee*'s crew were processed and interned, the cost to be borne by Germany. Sympathy for the German cause seemed to have evaporated, and the local newspapers, both in Buenos Aires and Montevideo, hinted at expectations that Langsdorff should have immolated himself and gone down with his ship like her eponym, Graf von Spee.

By the evening of Tuesday 19 December, Langsdorff had assured himself that his men were safe. He had addressed them that afternoon and made the point that he did not himself lack the personal courage to have died fighting a superior enemy, but that by doing so he would have caused his men to die with him. It was clearly a responsibility he could not face. In his closing remarks he referred to their attending the funerals of their shipmates 'a few days ago'. Then he added that: 'Perhaps you will be called upon to undertake a similar task in the future.' It was clear that he was ready to pay the price of his disobedience to his instructions and the loss of his ship.

That evening, with the crew moved into the Immigrants Hotel and the officers accommodated in the Argentine naval *Arsenale*, Langsdorff enjoyed a few drinks with his officers and members of the local German community. One or two of them perceptively guessed what was in the Captain's mind, but no one could stop him from going to his room and writing letters. He wrote to the German Ambassador at Buenos Aires, exculpating himself from the ineluctable necessity of having to destroy the *Admiral Graf Spee* 'after I had taken my ship into the trap of Montevideo'. It was, of course, a trap of his own making, but he added: 'a captain with a sense of honour cannot separate his own fate from that of his ship'. He concluded that he alone accepted responsibility for his ship's destruction and that he was 'happy that I can with my life prevent the casting of any imaginable shadow on the honour of the flag'; that he would 'meet my fate with firm faith in the cause and the future of the nation and of my Führer'.

After writing to his parents and his wife, telling her 'to be proud in her grief', in the small hours of 20 December, *Kapitän zur See* Hans Langsdorff shot himself. He was buried with full naval honours in Buenos Aires, his crew paying their respects as he had foretold, as did Captain Pottinger, representing the British prisoners confined aboard the German *Panzerschiff* during the battle.

Although Langsdorff had thought his death wrote *finis* to the tale, the game was not quite played out.

### 21 December, 1939–1946: 'Home Is the Sailor . . .'

The *Tacoma*, a ship of the Hamburg Amerika Linie, was unable to escape the consequences of her part in the fate of the *Admiral Graf Spee*. The Uruguayan government gave her master, Captain Hans Konow, notice to quit the port on 31 December on account of her acting as a German naval auxiliary by tendering to the German warship. Konow did not comply, so the *Tacoma*, her captain and his ship's company of thirty-eight were interned.

Across the great estuary in the following days, most of the *Admiral*

# Aftermath

*Graf Spee*'s 'rather haggard [. . .] and listless' ratings were removed from the Immigrants Hotel, split up and dispersed to various places of internment. In 1944 those who remained in Argentina were reunited on one site near Buenos Aires, to become prisoners of war in March 1945, when Argentina declared war on Germany. In 1946 most of the remaining officers and crew were repatriated in the *Highland Monarch*, the liner Langsdorff had intended intercepting in place of Harwood's cruisers. In a further irony, she was escorted by HMS *Ajax*. Some of the men took home Argentine wives, leaving 186 behind to settle in Argentina. Later they were rejoined by others who came back from a war-ravaged Germany so that about one-half of the *Admiral Graf Spee*'s crew finally settled in the Argentine.

Of her officers, Kay and a handful of departmental deputies remained to look after the crew during their internment. Many of the remainder escaped, it being their duty to do so. Police supervision was lax, local Germans assisted, as did some sympathetic Argentinians. Ascher got away first in January 1940 by air, a second group followed in March and a third, including Wattenberg, Klepp and Rasenack, in April. Most flew home using an Italian airline, though not always directly out of Argentina. After lying low and being hidden locally, Wattenberg flew to Chile and met two other crew members who had crossed the Andes on foot. They then flew back to Italy and on to Germany. Rasenack attempted to get home by sea, disguised as a Bulgarian commercial traveller. He was caught and interned by the American authorities in the Panama Canal Zone but the German consular officers obtained him a transfer onto a Japanese ship in which, eventually, Rasenack and a colleague arrived in a Japan not then at war with the Allies. From here they crossed to Korea, then part of the Japanese Empire, and by way of the Trans-Siberian Railway arrived in Moscow. There being a pact between Germany and Russia at this time, with the Russians having invaded and annexed eastern Poland, Rasenack arrived home on 1 September 1940. Some followed the same route, while others travelled by way of Paraguay and Brazil, despite protests and warnings by the British.

Ascher joined the *Bismarck* and was present at the sinking of HMS *Hood*, though he died with his ship when she was sunk by the Royal

# The Battle of the River Plate

Navy a few days later. Wattenberg was to escape from internment and become a successful U-boat commander, sinking a larger tonnage than his admired commander and the *Admiral Graf Spee* ever achieved, some 86,000 tons being credited to him. His submarine, *U-162*, was sunk 50 miles south of Barbados by HMSs *Quentin*, *Vimy* and *Pathfinder*, though Wattenberg escaped with his life. He was imprisoned in the United States, escaping again – but only briefly – from his camp in Arizona.

Langsdorff's adjutant, Kurt Diggins, also escaped to command U-boats, while other crew members survived equally extraordinary exploits, but the five naval reserve officers resumed civilian status and most were released accordingly. One of these, among those who reached Germany across Asia, was Langsdorff's chief prize officer, Herzberg. He joined another raider, this time the *Hilfskruizer* – or disguised armed merchantman – *Komet*, and died when she was sunk in the English Channel in October 1942.

For Langsdorff's British prisoners landed from the *Admiral Graf Spee*, Herzberg's prediction that for them 'the war was over' was far from the truth. After having a Christmas dinner at the British Legation 'or in other hospitable British homes in Montevideo', they were put aboard the first available ship heading for Britain where, in the words of Sir Eugen Millington-Drake, they were 'to resume their hazardous tasks as Merchant Navy officers in wartime'.

After the battle Harwood withdrew, despite his desire to make courtesy visits to Montevideo and Buenos Aires. The three cruisers, *Ajax*, *Achilles* and *Cumberland*, joined their battered consort *Exeter* in Port Stanley. Here all the ships' companies enjoyed their Christmas dinners. *Achilles* then went in search of the *Altmark* in Drake's Passage south of Cape Horn, afterwards rejoining Harwood's flag to make the postponed courtesy visits to Montevideo and Buenos Aires. The *Ajax* went to Montevideo where, as McCall reported, the visit was 'one triumphal progress' and 'wonderfully un-neutral'. The *Achilles*'s visit to Buenos Aires was more restrained, though Parry found it 'most astounding'. Ratings from the British cruiser encountered their opposite numbers from the *Admiral Graf Spee* on the streets, though these mostly passed off peaceably enough. Later in

# Aftermath

the war, as internment dragged, there were scuffles between German sailors and the apprentices from British merchantmen.

On their leaving the Rio de la Plata, Harwood briefly transferred his flag to *Achilles* before his new flagship, the old cruiser *Hawkins*, arrived at the end of January 1940. As they left for Auckland the 'Achilleses' – to use a contemporary collective noun for the ship's company – gave their chief 'a Maori farewell'.

The day after *Achilles* arrived in New Zealand to a heroes' welcome on 22 February, the crews of both *Ajax* and *Exeter* marched through London to a tumultuous response from their fellow countrymen. Bell's cruiser had been patched up in the Falklands, cosmetic disguises being added to cover the damage thanks to sheets of corrugated iron donated by the islands' farmers. She was escorted for part of her homeward passage by the *Renown* and *Ark Royal*: it was their only real connection with the battle. The *Exeter* had, moreover, been met at Plymouth earlier in the month by all the top brass from the Admiralty, including the First Lord, Winston Churchill. 'In this sombre, dark winter [. . .] the brilliant action of the Plate . . .' Churchill intoned, 'came like a flash of light and colour on the scene . . .' There was more in Churchillian vein: allusions to Drake and Ralegh, whose port Plymouth was. After leave, *Exeter*'s ship's company joined that of the *Ajax* for their triumphal parade through London. They marched past the King, past Churchill again, along with his Admiralty Board, and at the Guildhall Churchill made another speech, saying how in the middle of winter the victory had 'warmed the cockles of the British heart'.

It was a triumphal moment, and one that served its purpose as both a morale booster and as propaganda: Britannia still ruled the waves. Among the ranks of the Royal Navy marched six merchant masters, representatives of that other, rather more obscure British sea service. Their colleagues left behind aboard the *Altmark* were just then arriving home.

\*

# The Battle of the River Plate

Those 299 British seafarers remaining cooped up in the *Altmark* underwent weeks of privation, poor food and lack of exercise under Dau's harsh rule. They knew something had gone wrong when the mid-ocean meetings with the *Admiral Graf Spee* suddenly ended, and they could read what had happened on the faces of their gaolers. But the *Altmark* remained cruising in the South Atlantic until 22 January 1940, until, in due course, Dau received orders to head for home. Now the prisoners' own morale slumped when it appeared that they would all end up in a German prison camp.

The *Altmark* crossed the Equator on the 31st and Dau succeeded in avoiding any British warships, coming in sight of the snow-clad coast of Iceland on 11 February, entering the then neutral waters of Norway and embarking a Norwegian pilot a few days later. The *Altmark* began to head south, along the coast within territorial waters, being stopped off Trondheim and then off Bergen by two Norwegian patrol craft enforcing their country's neutral status. However, the Norwegian boarding officer, after a cursory inspection, accepted without apparent question the denials of Dau and his officers that the *Altmark* carried any prisoners of war. The assertions of the Germans were made against noises from below, where the prisoners – aware of what was going on – put up a racket to attract attention. The riot was quelled 'with hoses and the lights were turned out' although 'the Norwegians could not have failed to hear the noise we were making. We broke the hatch with iron bars and banged on this until we were repelled [. . .] but [. . .] it was useless.'

The fact that the *Altmark* bore naval colours and might therefore be regarded as a warship, was a slender excuse by which the Norwegian government might have justified their conduct, though they instructed the torpedo craft *Kjell* and *Trygg* to escort her. They might also have been nervous after a diplomatic row following the detention of the neutral American merchantman *City of Flint*, a prize of the *Deutschland* mentioned earlier. However, on the 16th the *Altmark* was spotted by an aircraft of the Royal Air Force. As dismissive of Norwegian neutrality as Dau, the Admiralty sent the cruiser *Arethusa* and a force of four destroyers under Captain Philip Vian to hunt the *Altmark* and she was eventually located by *Arethusa*, *Intrepid* and *Ivanhoe*.

# Aftermath

The attempts of the two destroyers to intercept the *Altmark* were frustrated by the *Trygg* and *Kjell*. Vian himself went in later with the *Cossack* and the captain of the *Kjell* challenged the British incursion, repeated the denial of the *Altmark* having British prisoners on board, stating the ship had been examined by the Norwegians the previous day, and said that she was authorized to sail through Norway's neutral waters. Vian's offer of a thorough and joint examination was rejected and this news was passed to the Admiralty, where the matter was raised at the highest level for a decision.

That evening Captain Philip Vian was sent in again in *Cossack*. Faced with *force majeure* Dau turned into the narrow waters of Jössing Fjord, where he attempted to evade Vian, thinking the navigational and diplomatic complexities would deter the British. Brushing aside the attempts of the Norwegians to block his approach, Vian headed into the narrow waters, rounding a bend to see the *Altmark* 'bows inshore, encased in ice, her great bulk standing black against the snow-clad mountains'.

HMS *Cossack*

Dau attempted to manoeuvre astern and ram the *Cossack*, but Vian and his 'imperturbable navigator Maclean' avoided a collision. As the two ships closed, Lieutenant Commander Bradwell Turner, leader of the boarding party, jumped across, followed by Petty Officer Atkins, who almost fell into the sea until Turner grabbed him and the two men caught a turn of a rope from *Cossack* round a set of bitts aboard the *Altmark*.

Like the cruiser action off the far distant Rio de la Plata, the boarding of the *Altmark* was redolent of a past age: Turner and his men carried small arms, including cutlasses. He reached the bridge and stopped the *Altmark*, which was at full speed as Dau tried to drag *Cossack* into shallow rock-strewn water and ground her. Vian, meanwhile, avoided this by letting go from the *Altmark* and going astern to leave Turner's party, all of whom had now boarded, to do their work. Dau surrendered, though his third mate, Schmidt, tried to keep the ship at full speed, and all might have ended there, had not one of the armed guards put on board by Langsdorff weeks earlier to look after the British prisoners, 'gratuitously shot Gunner Smith'. A fight began as the *Altmark*, crushing ice floes alongside close to the precipitous and rocky shoreline, allowed a few of these armed Germans to escape 'across the ice' and ashore, wrote Vian, from where they 'began to snipe the boarding party from an eminence [. . .] Silhouetted against the snow they made easy targets, and their fire was quickly silenced'.

Germans casualties were six killed and six wounded; the British party sustained only the wounded Smith. The German crew overcome, Turner broke open the hatches. 'Are any British there?' he shouted.

'Yes, we're all British!' they responded.

'Come on up then,' Turner cried. Whether or not he said: 'the Navy's here!' is uncertain, though it is fitting. The British merchant seamen, masters, mates, engineers, radio officers, sailors, trimmers and firemen – both British and Indian – had borne the brunt of the raiding cruise of the *Admiral Graf Spee*. At last the Royal Navy, their sure and certain bulwark, had caught up with them.

But even this was not quite the end. As Vian withdrew and *Cossack* steamed triumphantly down the fjord towards the open sea beyond, he left the *Altmark* humiliated and aground, but substantially intact. She returned to Germany and was returned to service under a new name, *Uckermarck*. Breaking the British blockade she made a daring voyage, reaching Japan with a valuable cargo. Ironically, she too blew up: safe in the port of Yokohama in November 1942 she fell victim to an error made in transferring her oil.

# Analysis

It is a curiosity of history that that memorable phrase, 'the Navy's here,' as the postscript of the Battle of the River Plate has left Vian's name as that of the hour's hero. Harwood, its architect, is long forgotten. The lives of both the principal protagonists in the Battle of the River Plate ended in tragedy. Langsdorff's death is the more obvious calamity, thought of as poignant – at least in the consensual opinion of popular and uncritical history. Notwithstanding this, Langsdorff's suicide was his only way out, for he had disobeyed orders and, far from covering himself in glory, had blown his ship up rather than fight to the finish, the outcome of which was not absolutely certain for those waiting for him off the Uruguayan coast.

Langsdorff had had the best and most innovative tools and machinery a renascent German industry, combined with an aggressive new political dynamic, could place in a naval commander's hands. Moreover, he had a young crew managed on progressive precepts and was a practitioner of an equivalently 'modern' leadership style.

Harwood – though his force was more potent than is generally regarded – nevertheless had under his command, ships that were the product of a legalistic conformity with treaty obligations and a Treasury strapped for cash. Moreover, at least one of his cruisers, *Exeter*, was in need of a refit and not in the best state of morale – going into action in a state described by one crew member as 'organized chaos'.

Yet, at the decisive moment it was Langsdorff who declined battle and Harwood who, after a momentary hesitation, maintained the hot pursuit with such dash that it deceived his opponent. It is this that demonstrates the plain fact that Harwood's leadership was based firmly on a priceless tradition in which the individual was subsumed by the savage collective will imbued by the Royal Navy, and by which means each man rose to the challenge of battle. Such ancient expectations were absent from the Third Reich's *Kriegsmarine* for all its pretensions. At the end of the day it is men who win battles, not ships, and the Royal Navy trained its officers from boyhood.

Harwood's personal tragedy was in its way the more poignant, for he was a victim of his own success, and that success was achieved by simply doing his duty with consummate professionalism. Victory off the Rio de la Plata had brought his name into prominence at a time when a battered Churchill was looking for iconic figures with which to stiffen and encourage British resistance to Nazi German successes elsewhere. Harwood's subsequent promotion to Commander-in-Chief in the Eastern Mediterranean was, despite his staff experience, beyond his ability. He was a fighting commander, a meticulous planner for offensive operations, and a front-line leader. He was not that combination of diplomat, administrator, motivator, leader and troubleshooter that was necessary in a British C-in-C in a remote yet vital theatre in which all arms, competing priorities and difficult allies were mixed with an uncertain indigenous political situation. Such men were rare indeed and Harwood cannot be blamed for his shortcomings, placed as he was by others, in such a *milieu*. His subsequent removal to an obscure command was insufficient to prevent the corrosive effect of stress. In August 1945 he was prematurely retired on medical grounds. He did not long enjoy this, dying in June 1950 at Goring-on-Thames.

One cannot escape the notion that Harwood was a man destined to bring the force of his intellect, the judgement and skills of his profession and the powers of his leadership to bear on an encounter between ships of war in the South Atlantic on 13 December 1939. All that preceded these tumultuous hours seems but a preparation, including his diplomatic sensitivity and finesse, and all his careful

# Analysis

exercising of his squadron. In this culmination he demolished the power of a puissant German warship and, at least for the time being, made the seas safer for the passage of British merchant ships in those waters. In this he was the epitome of the dashing British naval hero, not of the stature of a Nelson, but at one with the great cruiser-captains of the Nelsonic age, comparable with Edward Pellew, Richard Keats, Samuel Hood, Lord Cochrane, Robert Stopford, the Bowens and the Brentons.

His opponent, still remembered and even revered, is more complex. Langsdorff has spawned myths: he was not a Nazi, he wrapped himself in the old imperial German ensign before shooting himself, he did not give the National Socialist salute at the funeral of his dead shipmates; he did not kill a single man in the sinking of nine British merchant ships.

None of these assertions are quite as they seem, but mere tamperings with the truth. As for the notion that he was a humane commerce raider – a claim aided and abetted by the official British naval historian – the best that can be said is that luck prevented him from killing anyone. His shells were not discriminate, merely inaccurate. He was a German naval officer, a Party member and, withal, apparently a pleasant fellow, much admired by his officers and trusted – even loved – by his youthful crew, a crew which struck one Uruguayan newspaper reporter as mere boys.

Langsdorff's British captives spoke well of him but then merchant naval masters, in those first months of the war, found themselves in a difficult position. They had endured years of depression, many had suffered personal privation, and the war had given them employment. They were civilians and to others war was an interruption of their business. The initial observing of the so-called 'cruiser rules' by both Langsdorff and some of his young colleagues commanding U-boats induced for a while a mood between the hunters and the hunted akin to that expected of unfortunate professional encounters. Such was exemplified by Langsdorff's apologetic exchange with the *Clement*'s master: he was sorry, but war compelled him to sink Captain Harris's ship. Such meetings took place between other British masters, removed from their ships by U-boat commanders, and ended in gifts of cognac and directions to the nearest port for the lifeboats floating amid the flotsam of their torpedoed ship.

In Langsdorff's case, having these fellow sea captains confined in his ship, he took some of the British masters into his confidence; astonishingly so, at times. He and Patrick Dove became as close to friends as the acquaintance of war could make them, and Dove clearly admired Langsdorff. To what extent a later age would attribute such a juxtaposition as having been caused by the 'Stockholm syndrome' is a matter for conjecture. Friendship in war is perhaps a redeeming feature of the awful business, for all the anomaly of it, but such was the extent of examples of this apparent 'fraternization' that the Admiralty took alarm. The naval staff officers need not have worried. Soon the war took on a different aspect and matters changed between the hunters and their quarry, but in those first few weeks, something of the old ways persisted.

This suited Langsdorff. It cast him in a light he could accept, coming from his background of rural gentry, of continuity, tradition and quiet patriotism. The hints of chivalry, of gentlemen at war, the *Brüderbond* of the sea, of rules of engagement, all mattered to Langsdorff. It was a delusion, of course, a delusion as grand as that of war itself. Langsdorff lacked the killer-instinct of his opponent: Harwood's attack with torpedoes he could not credit as other than evidence that Harwood had heavy warships in support just over the horizon. Anything else was inconceivable. And having misjudged his opponents and discovered them more powerful than he at first thought, Langsdorff, having attacked fast to close the distance to pound them with his heavy guns, turned away. Some thought he did the right thing, and who amongst us who were not there can truly judge?

But if he made a tactical error, were his original orders – those which he disobeyed by engaging enemy naval forces – actually feasible? Did the German *Seekriegsleitung* not consider the reality of British sea power and its long arm? True the Royal Navy in 1939 was not what it had once been; true the *Altmark* made it as far as Norway,

# Analysis

but she did not reach Germany without interdiction, even though she was sneaking through the territorial waters of an intimidated neutral power. Could the *Admiral Graf Spee* have made it home with 50,000 tons of British shipping to her credit? Given the evidence of other German raiders, the answer is possibly – perhaps even probably – yes; but the matter was far from certain and the forces mustered against Langsdorff were considerable. In such circumstances it was foolish of the German High Command to impose such a stricture of avoiding contact upon a lone commander in the vast wastes of the ocean after a long cruise. Langsdorff was almost bound to have to pay the price of disobedience, for the odds of him being able to obey his orders to the letter were stacked against him.

Dau, in *Altmark*'s log, makes the perceptive comment that a submarine with a crew of forty could have done the work achieved by the *Admiral Graf Spee* and, as we have seen, Wattenberg proved the point in *U-162*. German experience with commerce raiders – even her disguised *Hilfskruizers* – was unhappy, for all their romantic adventurousness. It was even worse for her capital ships. Saving the *Bismarck*'s sinking of the *Hood*, the *Admiral Scheer*'s defeat of the Armed Merchant Cruiser *Jervis Bay* and the *Scharnhorst*'s and *Gneisenau*'s destruction of the *Rawalpindi*, neither of which were comparable in terms of weight of armour, and so forth, the exploits of the German *Kreigsmarine*'s most prestigious ships were not that impressive. Indeed the mighty *Tirpitz* did little more than bombard Russian coal mines at Spitsbergen. Only the *Admiral Scheer* could claim any real success, sinking 113,000 tons of Allied shipping during the cruise in which she engaged the *Jervis Bay* and her convoy. She also made a foray into the Kara Sea, sinking a Russian ice-breaker and bombarding Port Dickson in Siberia. All-in-all, with this single exception, the German capital ships were wasted through over-caution, and kept for much of the war in the Norwegian fjords, 'like chained dogs' as one officer complained. That Langsdorff wished to slip any such chains was, perhaps, a manifestation of his inner frustration and ambivalence. That he got it wrong and failed to destroy Harwood's squadron was the essence of his tragic failure.

# The Battle of the River Plate

Like their opponent, the *Admiral Graf Spee*, the British ships had their histories and their graveyards. After an extensive and modernizing refit, *Exeter* went east to reinforce the Far East Fleet as Japan entered the war. In February 1942 she was engaged by Japanese warships while part of an Allied force and hit again by shells, which damaged her boilers and caused her to fall out of a battle for the second time. In trying to escape west through the Sunda Strait she was cornered by overwhelming odds on 1 March. Attacked by cruisers and destroyers her new captain tried to scuttle her and while doing so the *Exeter* was hit by a torpedo fired by a Japanese submarine. She sank with heavy loss of life.

Once repaired the *Ajax* went out to the Mediterranean. She took part in the Battle of Matapan, operations off Crete and in Malta convoys. After bomb damage received at Bône was repaired, she returned to the Mediterranean and was later part of the force covering the D-Day landings in Operation NEPTUNE. Later in 1944 she provided accommodation for Churchill on his visit to Athens and, after escorting the *Highland Monarch* home from Buenos Aires in 1946, she was again part of the Mediterranean Fleet. Finally HMS *Ajax* returned home to be sold to Chile, but the deal failed and, in 1949, she was broken up. It was a year before Harwood's own death.

HMNZS *Achilles* was in action in the Pacific, where she received bomb damage which resulted in her being thoroughly modernized. She returned to the Pacific to serve in the newly constituted New Zealand Navy as part of the British Pacific Fleet, returning to Auckland in 1946 where she was placed in reserve. Then, in 1948, she was recommissioned as the INS *Delhi* and sent to join the newly independent Indian Navy under its loaned British Commander-in-Chief, Admiral Parry, her quondam captain. As *Delhi* she remained in commission until 1978, reverting to her former name in 1955 to star in Michael Powell's film of the Battle of the River Plate made off Malta. When she was finally broken up a gun turret and fire control director were acquired by the New Zealanders for their naval base in Auckland.

# Analysis

And Fallowfield's footnote to the action, HMS *Cumberland*, also lasted. Serving first in support of Arctic convoys, she ended the war in the Pacific. In 1951 she was converted to a gunnery trials ship and carried out this task until 1959 when she was scrapped. She too made a brief appearance in Powell's film.

By this time even the foretop of the *Admiral Graf Spee* had sunk beneath the muddy waters of the Rio de la Plata. Her role in Powell's film was played by the USS *Salem*, a heavy cruiser of vastly more imposing firepower than the *Panzerschiff*. As for the *Admiral Graf Spee* herself, she had burned for four days, after which McCall tried to secure what appeared to be high-frequency radio equipment in which he was assisted by one of the British team working on the development of radar who was specially flown out to Uruguay. Meanwhile Millington-Drake had been approached by a local merchant, Julio Vega-Helguara, who had in turn been sought out by Langmann who was seeking favours for wireless operators from the *Admiral Graf Spee*. Seeing an opportunity, the Uruguayan businessman thought the British might be interested in acquiring the wreck. For his part, eager to maintain the favour of the Uruguayans, Langmann was persuaded to sell the wreck to Vega-Helguara with a royalty on salvaged scrap. Vega-Helguara in turn asked Millington-Drake to finance the deal. Neither McCall nor his assistant could get near the wreck which was heavily guarded by the Uruguayans, and Vega-Helguara's deal offered a solution to an examination of the wreck and its equipment, specifically its grid antennae. Vega-Helguara now had the shipyard contractor Voulminot, two German officers and a British businessman named Kirkpatrick on side.

Negotiations with the Admiralty, an exchange of notes with the Uruguayans and some judicious palm-greasing by Vega-Helguara, eventually produced a deal in which the wreck was purchased in Vega-Helguara's name for £14,000. The next day a Uruguayan naval demolition party, probably directed by pro-German officers within the Inspectorate General of Marine, attempted to blow up the top of the control tower. The charge failed, but a warning that another attempt would be made followed in an attempt to head off the opposition. However, Vega-Helguara and a guard took formal

153

possession of the wreck on 1 March 1940. In due course another stranger arrived, this time a putative 'representative' of the ship-breaking firm of Thomas Ward, who boarded the ship and, on 6 and 7 March, climbed to the foretop. He reported that the *Admiral Graf Spee* was fitted with radar based upon a wavelength of 57cm and removed a section of the grid antenna and the cathode ray tube. Although German radar was less developed than that of the Allies and concentrated upon gunnery ranging rather than surface searching and locating, some technical detail was said to have derived from this acquisition, the remains of which are still in the Royal Navy's keeping. The real representative of Thomas Ward had had a difficult flight and had arrived a dangerously sick man. He failed to survive an operation to save his life and died on 6 March, described by Eric Grove as 'the final casualty of the Battle of the River Plate'.

Although further inspections were made by secret visitors and real representatives of Ward's, only about 1,000 tons of scrap was found to be salvable, while one demolition charge was discovered not to have exploded. Nevertheless the wrecked ship continued to promote projected salvage deals in quest of the guns, the undetonated torpedo head or the diesel engines. It was even thought possible that the entire ship might be lifted, though the cost was prohibitive and the scrap value inadequate to finance the attempt. Then the weather intervened to scotch these preposterous dreams. In mid-April a gale caused the ship to heel and resettle and the demolition parties succeeded in removing only a few parts: a light gun, a searchlight, and some other fittings and artefacts. A few documents were also recovered and some of the objects were sent to Britain. Others went ashore as trophies, but the salvage operations petered out.

The Battle of the River Plate was, for all its light and colour in those dark days, a grand delusion for the British too. Harwood's triumph supported the naval orthodoxy that believed the greatest threat to British commerce lay with the heavy and medium calibre guns of German commerce raiders, whether they belonged to *Panzerschiffs* or *Hilfsfkruizers*. The long search for the *Admiral Graf Spee* in a sense reinforced this view, presenting the Allied navies – but especially the

# Analysis

British – with a challenge which they succeeded in meeting at the cost of only nine merchantmen. Harwood's victory seemed to indicate the old lion could not only roar, but bite too, and when Vian ran down the *Altmark* in the Jössing Fjord it seemed the Royal Navy's writ still ran large across the seven seas; certainly in accomplishing the rescue and release of Dau's prisoners it had done its 'splendid bit'.

But all this obscured the real threat that lay awaiting Britain's foreign trade, overlaying its early exposure on the evening of the day war broke out when *Kapitänleutnant* Fritz-Julius Lemp had fired his torpedoes from *U-30* and sunk the Donaldson liner *Athenia*. Lemp too had disobeyed his orders, but he had – unwittingly – revealed how Germany might win the war at sea.

# Roll of Honour

HMS *EXETER*
Killed: 4 Officers
One Officer missing believed killed
50 Ratings killed in action
6 Ratings died of mortal wounds
One Rating missing, believed killed
Wounded: 3 Officers
20 Ratings

HMS *AJAX*
Killed: 7 Ratings

HMS *ACHILLES*
Killed: 4 Ratings

*Admiral Graf Spee*
Wounded: 61 Officers and Ratings
Died by his own hand: *Kapitän sur Zee* Hans Langsdorff

# Bibliography

All books published in London, except where indicated.

Aiken, A., *In Time of War*, Privately Published, Glasgow, 1980

Archibald, E.H.H., *The Fighting Ship in the Royal Navy*, Blandford Press, Poole, 1984

Bekker, C., *Hitler's Naval War*, Macdonald, 1974

Bennett, G.H. and R., *Survivors, British Merchant Seamen in the Second World War*, Hambledon Press, 1999

Dorling, H.T., *Blue Star Line, A Record of Service, 1939–1945*, The Blue Star Line, 1948

Dove, P., *I was the Graf Spee's Prisoner*, Cherry Tree Books, 1940

Frischauer, W., and Jackson, R., *The Navy's Here*, Victor Gollancz, 1955

Gray, E., *Hitler's Battleships*, Leo Cooper, 1992

Grove, E., *The Price of Disobedience*, Sutton, Stroud, 2000

Hardy, A.C., *Everyman's History of the Sea War*, Volume One, Nicholson and Watson, 1948

Hardy, A.C., *World Shipping*, Penguin Books, 1941

Haws, D., *Merchant Fleets 22, Glen and Shire Lines*, Privately Published, Hereford, 1991

Hinsley, F.H., Thomas, E.E., Ransom, C.F.G., and Knight, R.C., *British Intelligence in the Second World War*, Volume One, HMSO, 1979

Jordan, R., *The World's Merchant Fleets, 1939*, Chatham Publishing, 1999

Lenton, H.T., *British and Empire Warships of the Second World War*, Greenhill Books, 1998

# The Battle of the River Plate

Mallman Showell, J.P., (ed.), *Fuehrer Conferences on Naval Affairs, 1939–1945*, Greenhill Books, 1990

Millington-Drake, E., *The Drama of Graf Spee and the Battle of the Plate, A Documentary Anthology: 1914–1964*, Peter Davies, 1964

Pope, D., *Battle of the River Plate*, William Kimber, 1956

Rohwer, J. and Hummelchen, G., *Chronology of the War at Sea, 1939–1945*, Greenhill Books, 1992

Roskill, S.W., *The War at Sea*, Volume One, HMSO, 1954

Thomas, R.E., *Stowage: The Properties and Stowage of Cargoes*, Brown, Son and Ferguson, Glasgow, 1963

Trevor-Roper, H. (ed.), *Hitler's War Directives, 1939–1945*, Pan, 1966

Turner, L.C.F., Gordon-Cumming, H.R., and Betzler, J.E., *War in the Southern Oceans, 1939–1945*, Oxford, 1961

Vian, P., *Action this Day*, Frederick Muller, 1960

Warlimont, W., *Inside Hitler's Headquarters, 1939–1945*, Presidio, Novato, USA, 1964

Woodman, R., *The Real Cruel Sea*, John Murray, 2004

Young, J.M., *Britain's Sea War, A Diary of Ship Losses, 1939–1945*, Patrick Stephens, Wellingborough, 1989

# Index

Neither the battleship *Admiral Graf Spee* nor Captain Langsdorff have been indexed as they occur *passim*. The index is divided into two sections: Ships and General.

159

# Index

# Index